An Introduction
—— *to* ——
The Infinite Way Message *of* Joel S. Goldsmith

Elizabeth Parker

Elizabeth Parker
Loomis, CA
Elizabeth@goldsmithglobal.org

ISBNs: 978-1-7377902-0-4 (pbk); 978-1-7377902-1-1 (ebk)

Cover and book design by Mayfly Design

Library of Congress Catalog Number: 2021917081
First Printing: 2021
Printed in the United States of America

The Infinite Way® is a registered trademark.

Bible quotations are from the King James Version. In those instances where Joel Goldsmith does not cite the quotation exactly, Joel's words have been used.

Quotations from books by Joel S. Goldsmith are used with permission from the publisher, Acropolis Books, Inc.

Quotations from the class recordings of Joel S. Goldsmith are used with permission from the Estate of Joel S. Goldsmith.

Typographical emphasis is used in some quotations from the Goldsmith books for clarity, reading ease, or to highlight a key word or phrase.

CONTENTS

"AND YE SHALL KNOW THE TRUTH,
AND THE TRUTH SHALL MAKE YOU FREE."

~ JOHN 8:32

CHAPTER 1

JOEL GOLDSMITH AND THE INFINITE WAY

JOEL GOLDSMITH (1892 – 1964) said that he was a messenger who operated "under orders" from the Spirit within. He was inspired to bring forth a mystical spiritual message, which he called "The Infinite Way." While Joel has been acclaimed internationally as a spiritual teacher, author, and healer, he never took ownership of The Infinite Way message, saying that the principles revealed to him were not new. They had been revealed in the original teachings of Jesus and other spiritual masters, but eventually were lost or diluted. Joel saw himself as an instrument through whom the eternal principles of truth were re-revealed to the people of the twentieth century in the language of the day. He said:

"The principles are not new... the principles that are revealed in the Infinite Way are the result of a spiritual unfoldment that took place within me through many years of inner spiritual experiences and are found in the original message of all major teachings. Lao-Tzu of China, Buddha and Shankara of India, Jesus of Nazareth, and John of Patmos had the same experiences, not necessarily in the same form, but they all had revealed within them these same principles. So there is nothing new about them in that sense, except that the ideas are expressed in the language of the twentieth century."[1]

As a young man apprenticed to his father, who was in the import business, Joel traveled the world. He saw man's inhumanity to man and witnessed poverty and injustice, and he wondered where God was in this human scene.

" In the beginning, I had only one goal, and that was to discover why God is not in the human universe, why God does not stop wars or prevent them, why God does not stop or prevent murders, rape, arson, and suicides. Why is God not in this human picture? To find the answer to that question was my goal."[2]

In 1915, Joel's father was on a European buying trip and became seriously ill. Shortly after Joel learned that his father was dying, he had a chance encounter with a Christian Science practitioner, who offered healing help. Joel's father recovered completely. That experience prompted Joel to investigate Christian Science, seeking answers to his questions about the existence and nature of God.

After many successful years, Joel's import business began to fail. One day Joel became ill and sought help from a Christian Science practitioner. Not only was he healed of the physical problem that day; he had a complete change of consciousness. His lifestyle was permanently changed, and he found that he had the healing gift. Joel described the experience:

---

1. *God Formed Us for His Glory*: Chapter 2, "The Meaning of Living Spiritually."
2. *Living by the Word*: Chapter 4, "Easter: An Experience of Consciousness."

"Late in 1928, the Experience took place, that first God-experience. This Experience brought with it no message, no words, no rules, nor were any principles given: there was just an experience that could not be described. Whereas in one moment I was like every other human being, in the next moment, my body was well, and many undesirable human habits were gone. I found that a healing power was present and that I was on the threshold of a whole new life. The old life was dead; a new one had begun, but without a teaching, without any principles, without any laws—all this just because of an experience."[3]

People began to ask Joel for healing help, and one day he arrived at his business office to find that he had twenty-two phone messages. Not one was from a customer. Despite help from five different practitioners, Joel's business failed, and he found himself penniless. He joined the Christian Science Church, and for years he worked as a Christian Science healing practitioner and spiritual advisor. His healing practice flourished right away, but he did not understand *why* people were healed, and he began to search for the principles behind the healing. He immersed himself in a deep study of the spiritual writings and scriptures of the world.

Despite his success as a healer, Joel had difficulties in his personal life. Yet he did not experience discouragement, doubt, or fear, and as his spiritual awareness grew, life became increasingly harmonious.

Joel left the Christian Science Church in 1945. In 1947, he wrote his first book, *The Infinite Way*. He thought that after he finished the book, he would retire to a life of contemplation. However, the message he had put forth prompted people to seek

---

3. *Beyond Words and Thoughts:* Chapter 1, "Toward the Experience."

him out as a spiritual teacher. He held private classes on the mystical interpretation of the Bible, which were published later as the book *Spiritual Interpretation of Scripture*. Soon he had invitations for lecture tours and classes, and his ministry expanded. He traveled widely in the United States, Canada, the UK, Europe, Australia, New Zealand, and South Africa, teaching the message of The Infinite Way until his transition in 1964.

Joel Goldsmith never advertised, organized, or promoted his work, but in the years of his ministry, hundreds of thousands of readers and students around the world bought his books, many of which were translated into other languages. More than 1,250 hours of his class and lecture work were recorded. These recordings have been preserved and are available for purchase.[4]

NO ORGANIZATION FOR THE INFINITE WAY

Joel was beyond adamant that The Infinite Way never be organized. He believed that organization was the culprit that had put the veil on many messages of spiritual truth and obscured the original teaching. He was uncompromising in his stand that there never be memberships, obligations, codes of dogma, or structured leadership for The Infinite Way. He believed that students should be completely free to follow their own spiritual light with no binding ties to an organization. Joel never tried to build a following. He saw the message as a universal one and offered it to any seeker who found value in it. Yet he always respected their individual freedom.

---

4. All authentic recordings and transcripts are currently available at www.joelgoldsmith.com. Authentic recordings are also available on iTunes, and on www.joelgoldsmithstreaming.com, a subscription streaming service.

" In reading and studying The Infinite Way, . . . you are in no sense bound to it. You are, at all times, a free spiritual agent, free to come to us or to any of our students who are active in the work, but just as free at any time not to come—always free to find your own way. You have no obligations . . . and if The Infinite Way does not prove effective in your individual case, you are at liberty always to seek further until you do find the particular teaching which is yours."[5]

To this day, there is no organization, membership, obligation, or formal leadership associated with The Infinite Way. Spiritual seekers find The Infinite Way message on their own when they are ready for it, and often they find it in mysterious and wondrous ways.

There is an Infinite Way Office in Moreno Valley, California that is devoted to serving students by maintaining, preserving, and making available Joel's authentic class recordings, transcripts, and writings, and by offering other services. However, the Office has no organizational function.

JOEL GOLDSMITH'S INFLUENCE

Although Joel Goldsmith transitioned in 1964, his message continues to grow in popularity. Joel's work has inspired many spiritual teachers who consider him a key influence in their spiritual development.

Eckhart Tolle said, "A new generation of mature seekers, receptive to spiritual truth, is now discovering Joel Goldsmith's teachings, which have lost none of their relevance, aliveness and power. I foresee that those teachings will reach and impact even more people in the 21st century than during his lifetime. Joel

---

5. *The Contemplative Life*: Chapter 2, "Erasing Our Concepts of God, Prayer, and Grace."

Goldsmith's inspired and profoundly inspiring books represent a vital contribution to the spiritual awakening of humanity." Two of Joel Goldsmith's books are included on Eckhart Tolle's recommended reading list: *The Art of Meditation and A Parenthesis in Eternity*.

Gerald G. Jampolsky, M.D. called Joel "the ultimate teacher of spiritual wisdom," and **Marianne Williamson** said, "Joel Goldsmith has opened a door in my soul. He has helped me immeasurably in my search for peace."

During his distinguished ministry, **Dr. Wayne Dyer** spoke of Joel in this way: "I have an 8x10 picture of Joel Goldsmith on my writing table. I feel his presence with me every day. I consider Joel to be one of my most important teachers. His wisdom guides me in all of my work."

CHAPTER 2

WHY THIS BOOK?

ANYONE WHO BECOMES INTERESTED in the work of Joel Goldsmith finds a rich legacy of over fifty books and more than 1,250 hours of recorded class work. Collectively, the books present The Infinite Way message, and the recorded classes provide the opportunity to hear and learn from the messenger himself. Faced with this vast treasure of resources, where does a newcomer begin? How do you navigate this enormous sea of material?

Upon reading their first Goldsmith book or hearing their first recorded class, many students resonate with it right away. In their joy and delight at finding this message, they go on to other books and recordings with ever-increasing appreciation for the beauty of the teaching. Many feel the "rightness" of it. But despite much study, years later they may find themselves hard pressed to describe the essence of the message in clear and simple terms. This was my experience.

My discovery of The Infinite Way came in a startling way. I was living in Berkeley, California, exploring the smorgasbord of spiritual paths offered in the Bay Area in the early nineteen-eighties. From time to time, a path would bring temporary enthusiasm and the hope that I had found "the one" for me. But ultimately, I was disappointed and moved on.

One day it came to me to stop my outward pursuit and just sit quietly in my home and meditate, holding the question

"What is God?" I followed this interior guidance day after day, but nothing came. Even so, I persisted. One day, out of the clear blue, this came to me: "God is the substance of all form." It made no sense to me; I did not understand what it meant. Nonetheless, I continued the meditations: "What is God?" Again it came: "God is the substance of all form."

Shortly thereafter, I was browsing the books in a metaphysical bookstore, and I was drawn to one book that stood out as if lit in neon lights. It was *God, the Substance of All Form*, by Joel S. Goldsmith. Right away, I knew that this book was for me. Later when I began to read it, I could not stop. I did not understand much of what I was reading, but I felt the truth of it. It resonated with me as nothing else had. I knew that I had found my spiritual home.

I returned to the bookstore and purchased all the books they had by Joel Goldsmith, and I read and read and read. Sometime later, I discovered Joel's recordings, and I listened and listened and listened. Yet if someone asked me the simple question, "What is The Infinite Way?" I fumbled. I felt as though I was working with many puzzle pieces but did not have the picture on the cover of the puzzle box to guide me in putting them together. It was many years before that picture emerged and I had a clear view of the message.

Joel himself observed that many students have difficulty finding the principles in the books.[1] He said that students who have lived ten or twelve years with the books would gradually begin to perceive specific principles, but he also said that students could make faster progress if a teacher identified and repeatedly presented those principles. In my own study, often I wished for some sort of introduction that laid out the principles and practices—the "bones" of the message—so that I could put

---

1. Recording 510B: 1963 Instructions for Teaching The Infinite Way, "Instructions to Teachers and Practitioners."

"flesh" on those bones as I went along. In other words, I wanted the cover picture on the puzzle box.

A tourist map of a great city shows you the basic layout of the city, locates the city's major features, and helps you find your way. This book is the "map" that came into focus for me after many years as I sought to "find the pearls" and catch the essence of The Infinite Way message. I did not set out to write a book. At first, I had just an ongoing collection of quotations that I found most helpful as I studied, together with notes on the insights that came to me in contemplation and meditation. Later, as I worked with students, I used these materials to help them make their study and practice more effective. Eventually, I was led to compile them into this book.

In composing the book, I have functioned somewhat as a curator, selecting and arranging passages from Joel's work to create and illustrate the "map" as I see it. Should you choose to study The Infinite Way message, a unique map may come to light for you that may differ from this one. Even so, I share the one that emerged from my experience, because I believe that as you begin, it can serve as a basic framework, a context for exploring and studying the many Infinite Way books and recordings. This book answers basic questions such as:

- What is The Infinite Way?
- What is the premise of the message?
- What is the purpose of the message?
- What spiritual principles are taught in the message?
- What are the recommended practices?
- What is spiritual healing?
- What is the mysticism of The Infinite Way?
- How might I study the message of The Infinite Way?

Even if you have a good map of a city, you must visit the museums, eat in the restaurants, and spend time at the historic sites and other attractions to fully experience the richness of the city. Similarly, you have to delve wholeheartedly into the books and the recordings and consciously engage in the practices to experience the fullness of The Infinite Way message. In other words, when you finish this book, you are really at the start of your journey.

If this book resonates with you, and you choose to study the message further, it is my deepest wish that your study will be more effective and fulfilling for having had this introduction.

FORMAT OF THE BOOK

In one of his classes, Joel told students to "read the books in a different way than you have before."[2] He recommended that they take one topic, search in all their books for chapters or sub-chapters on that one topic, and study just those sections. He believed that approaching a topic in this way would result in "catching the idea," on that topic. This book follows that recommendation by focusing on one idea, principle, or practice at a time.

The book uses many quotations from Joel so that the reader can "hear" from Joel himself. Except for short quotations embedded in an explanatory paragraph, quotes from Joel are indented, with the first letter of the first word set in large, bold font. In keeping with convention, if there is more than one paragraph in the quotation, additional paragraphs begin with an opening quotation mark, and only the final paragraph in the quotation is closed with quotation marks. Ellipses (three dots) indicate that some words have been omitted from a quotation. [Bracketed] words in a quotation are words added for clarification or reading ease.

Footnotes for book quotations provide the title of the book, and the chapter number and title in which the quote appears.

---

2. Recording 643A: 1956 Johannesburg Closed Class, "The Anointed of God."

Over the years, many of the books have been reprinted several times, and page numbers vary from edition to edition, so specific page numbers are not given. Nearly all references are to books by Joel, so those references do not cite Joel as the author. If there is a reference to a book by someone other than Joel, the author's name is given.

Recordings are referenced by number, year, class, and session. A "class" refers to a group of teaching sessions given by Joel in a specific location in a specific year. Joel's class sessions were first recorded on reel-to-reel audiotapes that had two sides, referred to as "Side A" and "Side B," so one reel-to-reel tape included the recordings for two class sessions, one on each side. Each two-sided audiotape was assigned just one number, so the two class sessions on that one tape were referenced by the tape number, followed by "A," which designated the first side, or "B," which designated the second side. Generally, the recording numbers reflect the chronology of the classes.

With few exceptions, classes are designated as open, closed, practitioner, or special. An open class was open to anyone who wished to attend. A closed class was for students who had read some of the books and were familiar with the teaching. A practitioner class was for advanced students, most of whom who were teaching, doing healing work, or leading study groups. A *special* class was usually an invitation-only private class.

When a recording is cited in this book, the citation gives the number of the recording, the title of the class, and the title of the session within the class. For example, the citation "Recording 468A: 1962 Chicago Closed Class, 'Discovery of My Self'" means:

- The number of the recording is 468A.
- The class was given in 1962 in Chicago, and it was a closed class.
- The recording is the session in the 1962 Chicago Closed Class that was named "Discovery of My Self."

THE LANGUAGE OF THE INFINITE WAY MESSAGE

In the books and recordings, you will read and hear words such as "God," "prayer," and "Christ," as well as other words commonly used in other teachings and religious traditions. Sometimes when people see or hear these words, instantly they interpret them through an orthodox lens and hastily conclude that this message is "more of the same" and not for them. But in The Infinite Way, these words do not have orthodox meanings. For example, many people read the word "Christ" and automatically think that it means Jesus. They may read the word "God," and think of an old man with a beard somewhere in a heaven, or they may think of a man on a cross. They may read "prayer," and think of petitioning God for something. But in The Infinite Way, these terms have vastly different meanings. As Joel said,

" When you first embark on a spiritual or religious way of life, questions regarding the meaning and use of certain words will inevitably arise. You cannot speak without using words, and as you know from consulting any unabridged dictionary, the same word may have many meanings and sometimes not even similar meanings, depending on how it is used. When it comes to religious terminology, this is even more true because people of many different religions use the same words, such as a word like 'God' . . . But if you were to ask a Roman Catholic about God, you would have one answer; from a Protestant another answer; from a Hebrew still another; from a Vedantist a quite different one; and those following the teachings of Shankara or Zen Buddhism would give even other meanings for 'God.' Yet they all use the word 'God,' and it means something different to each one.

"In metaphysics, the word 'Christ' has a different meaning from its meaning in orthodoxy, and the word 'prayer' is hardly recognizable from its dictionary meaning. Prayer to most people is a petition to God for something. To other people it is an affirmation of truth. To still others it is wordless, but with inner thought, and then to others it is wordless and without thought. So 'prayer' has different meanings for different persons. . . .

"As you study the various approaches to truth, you will find that the teachers use the same words, but that each approach gives to those words their own special meaning. So it is in The Infinite Way. We do not always agree with others on the meaning of words, and others do not agree with us. That is understandable. The main thing is that we ourselves understand what we mean when we use certain words, statements, thoughts, or truths."[3]

Joel said that The Infinite Way writings and recordings use the language of Christian mysticism simply because his personal search was always in the direction of Jesus Christ. But the *principles* taught in the message are universal. As Joel once commented: "I could rewrite every one of these books in the language of Hebrew mysticism, or Oriental mysticism—either Hindu, Chinese, or Japanese."[4]

Joel advised students not to get stuck in the particular words used to convey a spiritual idea, but to "catch the spirit" behind the words. If you are willing to set aside your assumptions about specific words and read the books and hear the classes with an open mind, you will "catch the spirit" and come to understand new and often more profound meanings for those words.

---

3. *The Only Freedom*: Chapter 4, "Progressive Unfoldment."
4. Recording 300B: 1960 Los Angeles Open Class, "Foundation of The Infinite Way."

PUTTING THE WORK IN CONTEXT

Joel Goldsmith shared the spiritual revelations that came to him with many thousands of students who attended his lectures and classes. Yet different audiences were in different states of spiritual readiness and drew forth lessons that aligned with their state of consciousness. For example, what came through in a class for longtime students was often deeper than what came through in an introductory lecture.

Most of Joel's books draw on his classwork, so some book chapters reflect the more foundational classes, while others reflect the deeper classes. A new student reading the books in a random fashion might get the mistaken impression that Joel says one thing in one book and something different in another. This can be confusing unless you understand that the differences are not contradictions, but that they reflect the range of depth that came forth in classes for audiences at different levels of spiritual development.

Joel had a unique teaching style. He did not prepare lessons. His class preparation was deep, intensive meditation over the days or weeks preceding a class. When Joel took the platform, he opened his consciousness to Spirit. He said that the spiritual impartations that came through in classes often were new to him, and that he was hearing them for the first time along with the students. Sometimes he was inspired to speak about an aspect of the message in a new way. So, while the principles he taught did not vary, the depth, breadth, and manner of his presentation evolved over the duration of his ministry. Again, if you do not know this, you may be puzzled by what seem to be different explanations of the same idea. This book is designed to help new students establish a foundation that enables them to understand and accommodate these variations.

THE ATTITUDE OF THE STUDENT

Joel never asked anyone to accept what he said just because he said it. He encouraged students to ponder his teaching and listen within to see if they felt a "rightness" about it and to apply the principles in their own lives to see if they could demonstrate them.

> " I don't ask anyone to have faith in what I say. I merely say it and leave it with you to ponder, to meditate upon, and to get the answer from within your own being. It wouldn't do you any more good to accept blindly what I say than to accept blindly the religious beliefs that you have accepted for centuries. To have a blind faith in any religious teaching is next to a waste of time. Faith must be founded on an *inner* assurance of truth. There must be something within an individual to say, 'This is it,' or else they're just following the blind blindly." [5]

SIGNS OF THE TIMES

Joel's Infinite Way ministry spanned the nineteen-forties, -fifties and -sixties. You may find words or references in the books and recordings that reflect the social consciousness of those years, which was different in many ways from the social consciousness of today. However, these occasional remarks do not bear on the core of the message, so it is helpful to simply regard them as signs of the times.

The message of The Infinite Way has been in the world for over seventy years. Thousands upon thousands of students have contemplated and practiced the principles revealed in the message, thereby further establishing them in consciousness. As a

---

5. Recording 300B: 1960 Los Angeles Open Class, "Foundation of The Infinite Way."

result, it easier for students today to understand the message, practice it, and reap the benefits. In turn, their dedicated study and practice will give the message still deeper roots, benefiting those yet to come.

CHAPTER 3

WHAT IS THE INFINITE WAY?

"THE INFINITE WAY" is the name that Joel Goldsmith gave to the message that he taught around the world for nearly twenty years. *The Infinite Way* is also the title of his first book. But beyond the name and the book title, what is The Infinite Way?

The Infinite Way is a spiritual path that begins with a teaching, becomes a way of life, and culminates in an experience.

As a *teaching*, The Infinite Way presents specific spiritual principles that were revealed to Joel Goldsmith, experienced and proven by him, and presented in his books and recorded classes. Joel referred to these principles as "the correct letter of truth," and he emphasizes that learning the correct letter of truth through the books and the classes is an essential first step on the spiritual path.

The Infinite Way becomes a *way of life* when you apply the spiritual principles in daily living and engage in the recommended practices. This way of life purifies and elevates your state of consciousness, and eventually the principles "drop from the head to the heart" and become your own realized consciousness. You can attest personally to the truth of them.

At some point, you enter the *experience* of Truth, which has been called by many names—"the God-experience," "Self-realization," "the experience of the Christ," "Christ Consciousness," and "illumination," among others. Ultimately, The

Infinite Way is an experience of God, of the truth of your real identity, or what Joel called your Christhood, the Christ of your being. In that experience, you live entirely by Grace.

When Joel used the term "Christ," he was not referring to Jesus. He was referring to the divine Presence within every individual, the true Self, the spirit of God in man, or what Jesus spoke of as "the kingdom of God within you."[1] Jesus is called "Jesus Christ" or "Christ Jesus" or "Jesus the Christ" because he was fully awake to this divine Presence within him, and he lived from that identity.

Consciously or unconsciously, many think that the experience of God must be something so awesome, so astonishing and spectacular, that it could never happen to them. Yet Joel taught unequivocally that God is *already* the true Self of individual being. So, at some level we are already "experiencing" that truth, but we are not *consciously* experiencing it; we are not *consciously* aware of our own true identity. The Infinite Way path is not about gaining something that we do not already have, but about removing whatever stands in the way of our *consciously* experiencing the truth that already exists.

The Infinite Way message offers to guide the spiritual seeker from a teaching, to a way of life, to an experience. It is an invitation to learn to live in a new way, a way that leads ultimately to a life that is effortless, harmonious, and perfectly fulfilled, and a life that serves to uplift the consciousness of mankind.

A HELPFUL FRAMEWORK: THE FOUR Ps

One way to look at The Infinite Way message is through the four Ps— the *premise*, the *purpose*, the *principles*, and the *practices*.

---

1. See Luke 17:21.

The First P: The Premise of The Infinite Way

The premise of any spiritual teaching is the fundamental truth on which the teaching is based. This is how Joel described the premise of The Infinite Way:

" The basic premise of our entire work, the one on which all of this work is founded, is that God constitutes individual consciousness. This really is the foundation stone of our entire work."[2]

" The premise [is] that God is the reality of your being, that all that is true of God is true of you, and that only that which is true of God is true of you . . ."[3]

" The foundation of this teaching is that every person individualizes all the qualities and activities of God—all intelligence, eternal life, all love, all truth. Not one quality is lacking in any individual."[4]

" God has already expressed Himself, or Itself, as your very being. God is your Self, and that is why you are already infinite. . . . God is individual consciousness . . . God is the soul of you, the spirit of you. God is the substance of your being. God is the law of your being, and even your body is the temple of the living God. Therefore, in your oneness with God, you are already infinite, complete, perfect."[5]

---

2. Recording 324B: 1960 Chicago Open Class, "God as My Being—A Meditation."
3. *The Master Speaks*: Chapter 15, "Meditation and Healing."
4. *Conscious Union with God*: Chapter 2, "Teacher, Student, and Teaching."
5. Recording 137B: 1956 Melbourne Closed Class, "The Principles of 'As' and 'Is,' continued."

To be clear, this is not to say that God is the reality of your *humanhood*, but of your *true identity*. Chapter 5, "The Nature of Individual Being," will explain this further.

The Second P: The Purpose of The Infinite Way

A purpose is the reason for which something is done or created, or for which something exists. Joel made clear the purpose of The Infinite Way message:

" The entire purpose of the teaching of The Infinite Way is to bring seekers of God back to the original teaching of Jesus Christ and to the teaching of other mystics who have always taught that, since the kingdom of God is within you and me, it is possible through prayer, meditation, and communion to become consciously aware of this divine Presence and to experience this Presence as the very Christ or Son of God within us, actually living our lives for us."[6]

" The purpose is first of all to reveal your true identity; to reveal that you are not mortals; you are not sinners; you are not material man who was born and will die. That is not your true identity. That is a false sense of you, which you entertain because it is a universal belief. You have accepted it. Merely by being born, you've accepted the universal belief about yourself that you are something separate from God. And so, the major purpose of this message is to reveal to you again that which has been revealed several times in the religious history of the world: 'Know ye not, ye are children of

---

6. *The Heart of Mysticism: Volume 5, The 1958 Infinite Way Letters:* Chapter 6: June, "Security Through God-Realization."

God, and if children, then heirs, and if heirs, joint heirs with Christ.'[7]

"Now, once that has been revealed to you and something within you responds and says, 'Oh yes, I can feel the truth of that. I always knew I was something better than just flesh and blood and bones. I always knew there was something more to me than even my human conduct. I've always known there was something better, something deeper within me,' . . . well then, you have intellectually accepted it and in a measure perceived it. And now the *purpose* of this message is to help the student achieve the *realization*. . . .

"You have that mind which was also in Christ Jesus, but you are not in *conscious realization* of it. And so, the Christ mission is first of all to acquaint you with the fact that you already have that mind that was in Christ Jesus, and then secondly, to help you achieve the conscious realization and demonstration of it."[8]

The Third P: The Principles of The Infinite Way

A principle is a fundamental truth that serves as the foundation for a body of knowledge. Joel referred to the spiritual principles of The Infinite Way as "the correct letter of truth." While Joel said that the letter of truth is not Truth Itself, but rather "the truth *about* the Truth," he emphasized that learning the correct letter of truth is an essential first step on the path that leads to the experience of Truth, or the experience of God.

Joel identified two aspects to The Infinite Way message:

---

7. See Romans 8:16-17.
8. Recording 9B-2: 1952 New Washington Series, "Greater Works."

"There is that which we call 'the letter of truth,' the foundational understanding; or truth that can be intellectually known, can be intellectually stated. It gives us a foundation upon which to stand. . . .

In addition to the letter of truth, there is a part of this teaching that consists of . . . at least three-quarters of our work, and that has nothing to do with the letter at all. It has to do with the actual experience of the Christ. It has to do with an actual experience of God. Now, the value of the correct letter is that it clears the way for the experience to take place, an experience that very seldom can take place until there is a correct background of the letter."[9]

Chapter 10 elaborates on these two aspects of the message, but the point to catch here is that knowing the correct letter of truth must be the first step.

Principles in The Infinite Way Message

Students who are new to The Infinite Way soon catch the idea that there are specific spiritual principles in the message, and that it is important to know these principles. Some even start a list, and every time they read or hear Joel say, "this is a principle," they write it down. This method reflects sincere intent but can result in a very long list of principles, which can obscure the simplicity of the message. As Joel said:

"When we undertake the study of The Infinite Way, it must seem to be a difficult subject, one not easy to encompass. The reason is, we are always hitting up against more and more principles. Every time we

---

9. Recording 86A: 1954 Honolulu Closed Class, "Fifth Chapter of Matthew."

read a book or every time we hear a tape, there are more principles and we wonder if we are ever going to get to the end of it.

"As a matter of fact, it is not quite that way. There are not many principles revealed in the message of The Infinite Way. What seems to make it so involved is that each principle requires so many different ways of hearing and reading before we actually attain the consciousness of it. . . . [For example,] you can go through the Infinite Way writings and spend months just on the nature of God. This is not because there are a lot of principles to learn. There is only one principle—the principle of the Nature of God. However, there are hundreds of facets of that Nature . . ."[10]

Knowing the principles, or the correct letter of truth, is important for several reasons. First, if we harbor any mistaken beliefs, we have to release them, but if we do not know the correct letter of truth, we have nothing with which to replace them. Second, we must know the principles so that we can work with them, practice them, and validate them for ourselves. Finally, the correct letter of truth is the foundation for developing the mystical consciousness, or the full experience of the presence of God. Joel said, "There is no way to develop the . . . Christ-consciousness without an understanding of the basic points."[11]

Four Major Principles

While Joel taught the principles throughout the books and classes, a new student may not happen to find a place in which Joel stated the core principles simply and specifically. Students

---

10. *The Spiritual Power of Truth*: Chapter 9, "God and Error."
11. *A Message for the Ages*: Chapter 11, "Guidelines for Spiritual Unfoldment Through The Infinite Way."

may study for a long time before the key principles of the teaching stand out in stark relief.

A review of the entire body of Joel's work clearly reveals that he focused on four major principles. He elaborated on the many aspects of these four, and he used the term "principle" more liberally, but often he stated that there are four major principles:

1. The nature of God
2. The nature of individual being
3. The nature of error
4. The nature of prayer.

Sometimes Joel cited three foundational principles; sometimes he cited two; and other times he cited all four. Nonetheless, looking across the totality of Joel's work, it is clear that he consistently returned to these four principles.

" Now, the day must eventually come to our students, when they know the **nature of God**, the **nature of prayer**, the **nature of individual being**, and the **nature of error**. Those four things must constitute the basis of their knowledge of the letter of truth."[12]

Chapters 4, 5, 6 and 7 of this book elaborate on these four principles.

The Fourth P: Infinite Way Practices

Joel taught specific practices that help to build a *realized* consciousness of the principles. These practices include:

- Practicing the Presence
- Contemplation
- Meditation and prayer

---

12. Recording 121A: 1955 Kailua Study Group, "Experience of the Christ."

- Studying The Infinite Way writings and recordings
- Studying scripture
- Practicing the principles in daily life
- Associating and communing with others on the path

Each of these will be explained in Chapter 8, "Infinite Way Practices."

THE INFINITE WAY IS DIFFERENT

Joel recognized that the truth expressed in The Infinite Way message was not new and had been known by spiritual masters for thousands of years. Yet he also knew that The Infinite Way message was different from other teachings of his time, just as it is different from other teachings today. How is it different?

Different Starting Point

The message of The Infinite Way has a different starting point, which is that God constitutes your individual being, and that the kingdom of God is *already* established within you. As Joel said, "That which I am seeking, I already am."[13] This is not a message that starts with a human being and works to make the human become spiritual. The Infinite Way is based on the premise that you already *are* a perfect spiritual being, and that the work is to make that truth *real* in your experience by dispelling whatever may be concealing it.

" While I do not claim that the truth expressed in The Infinite Way has not at some time or other been included in the teachings of the great sages and seers . . . the purpose of this teaching is probably differ-

---

13. *The Heart of Mysticism: Volume 4, The 1957 Infinite Way Letters:* Chapter 8: August, "Your Names Are Written in Heaven."

ent from almost any other teaching. The Infinite Way stands wholly and completely on the revelation of Jesus as given in the Gospel according to John. . . . 'I[14] am life eternal; I am the way, the truth, and the light.[15]' 'I am the resurrection'[16]—not 'I will be resurrected;' not that there is some kind of a law of God which is going to act upon me; but I am the resurrection. 'I am the bread'[17]—not 'I will be supplied with bread,' but I am the bread; I am the water; I am the wine. When you stand on that, you stand on the revelation that you are infinite spiritual consciousness, infinite spiritual life itself, . . . including within your own being every activity of Being."[18]

Different Goal

Unlike many other paths, the goal in The Infinite Way is not to change human conditions, not to gain better health, more wealth, better relationships, or even more knowledge of truth. The goal is to *experience the presence of God*. Human conditions do change as a result of that experience, but the improved conditions are not the goal on this path. They are the "added things." The Infinite Way follows the teaching of Jesus to "seek ye first the kingdom of God."[19]

" **N**ow, in ordinary religious work, the end and object is to attain some measure of better humanhood, . . . which is a fine thing to attain. But it is not the work of The Infinite Way to go into that phase of life at

---

14. Whenever the word "I" is set in a different font type within a quotation, it refers to the true divine identity of an individual.

15. John 14:6.

16. John 11:25.

17. John 6:35.

18. *Conscious Union with God:* Chapter 7, "Making the Adjustment."

19. Matthew 6:33.

all. In The Infinite Way, the object is to attain a measure of that mind that was in Christ Jesus and then let It do with us what It will."[20]

"The primary purpose of our work is to bring forth our true identity as Spirit, as God made manifest, as Life, individually expressed in all of life's harmony and perfection. We, in our work, do not attempt just to turn sick people into well people, or poor people into rich people. Improving humanhood is not our main object. The fruitage of our work is improved health and supply, but the improvement of material conditions is not its prime object. These are only the 'signs following.' The primary object is to reveal God as individual being, to reveal that there are not God *and* man, but that there is only God, God appearing as individual you and individual me, to reveal that 'I and my Father are one.'[21] There are not both a God *and* you, but since God is infinite, and God is all, then God must express Itself, manifest Itself, *as* you and *as* me."[22]

"The Infinite Way never had any intention of being anything but a mystical message, a message revealing the possibility of attaining its goal of conscious union with God, and the means of attaining it. During all these years the writings and the recordings bear witness to this: The Infinite Way is not a system of attaining improved humanhood; it is the attaining of the Christhood."[23]

---

20. Recording 65B: 1954 Honolulu Lecture Series, "Meditation on One Power."
21. John 10:30.
22. *The Master Speaks*: Chapter 11, "The Allness of God."
23. *Consciousness Transformed*: September 14, 1963, "There Is Only One God Consciousness."

Different Perspective on Teachers

At first, students learn The Infinite Way message from the books, the recordings, and teachers, but Joel explained that when students are ready, they are taught from within. He said that the real function of a teacher is to free the student from the teacher.

"Please remember this: This Infinite Way message is unique in that it does not teach you to rely on the teaching, the books, or the revelator. The Infinite Way has a teacher and books and teachings only for the purpose of leading you back to the kingdom of God within your Self, so that you may be taught of God. . . . Remember that we in The Infinite Way are not trying to develop a following, nor are we trying to develop fame or fortune. I, at least, and some of the teachers who have learned from me, are trying (sometimes even against the pressure of students) to bring to you the awareness that you have just as much access to the kingdom of God as we have. If you want to heal, you can do as much as any of us have done. That is the message of The Infinite Way."[24]

Complete Original Message

The original Infinite Way message as taught by Joel Goldsmith is captured in a complete collection of writings and recordings, which is available to students today. Also, the message is complete in the sense that it provides specific spiritual principles as well as practices for spiritual development. The spiritual principles that constitute the letter of the message and the practices that bring those principles to life in everyday experience are captured and detailed in more than fifty books, over 1250 hours of recorded classes, and transcripts for those classes. Students

---

24. *Consciousness Transformed*: April 19, 1964, "Experience God."

can learn from the revelator himself. Speaking of the value of original recordings, Joel said,

"Today nobody has to trust to their memory. We don't even have to trust to a stenographer, because . . . the message is taken down complete, full, at the very moment that it is spoken, so that there isn't a single word missing, and the inflection of the voice carries its meaning."[25]

Practical Message

Some people believe that the spiritual way of life is not practical, or that it can only be lived successfully by those who live away from the world. Joel did not think so, and he presented his message as exceedingly practical.

"This means of spiritual living does not result in frustration and it is not escapism. It is the most practical way of living in a practical universe that you can possibly know, because when you have attained the ability to live through this realization of the Christ, live it and have it with you on all occasions, you'll find how practical it is in helping you meet your bills, and keeping your body well, and keeping your home in order. Oh, you'll be surprised, when once you see it operate, how practical it is."[26]

No Organization and Individual Freedom

Unlike many spiritual paths, The Infinite Way has no organization to join, no memberships, and no dogma that students must

---

25. Recording 278B: 1959 Manchester Closed Class, "Impersonalization Illustrated."
26. Recording 705A: 1955 Johannesburg Closed Class, "The Inner Meaning."

accept. Joel wanted students to be free to come to the message and equally free to leave.

" We have no organized activity in any form—no memberships, no dues, no loyalties, nothing. There is just the presentation of this way of life which has been given to me, revealed to me, and which I am presenting, and anyone who would like it is welcome to it. . . . Never under any circumstances or at any time are they required to leave anything or anybody or to join anything or anybody, because the essence of this work is freedom, man's individual freedom under God, man's individual freedom to find his own religious way, his own way of life without obligation. . . . They are free to come and free to go, and the only union there is between us, the only bond there is, is the spiritual one of our mutual love of God and love of work in this venue. Aside from that, there are no ties."[27]

" Each student is free to study, to meditate, to unite with us in our spiritual activities, and at any time that he discovers that this is not his way, he can leave with blessings, with love, and with the same degree of friendship that we had while we were working together because no ties have been broken."[28]

Joel even went as far as to say that students should not accept the message on blind faith.

---

27. Recording 375A: 1960 Melbourne Closed Class, "The Nature of Spiritual Attainment."
28. *Seek Ye First*: Chapter 2, "The Spiritual Goal."

" I don't believe in blind faith, and it is always my hope that when a principle is presented in the message of The Infinite Way, the students will eventually come to the *realization* of that principle, not the acceptance of it because it says so in The Infinite Way; not because Joel says it."[29]

" You must remember that in all this Infinite Way teaching, I am not asking anyone to believe what I'm teaching. I'm asking them to live it and demonstrate it. After they have demonstrated, they believe it. Before they have demonstrated, I don't see how they can believe it, regardless of how much faith they may have in me or in God, for that matter. What comes to you as demonstration is what carries your true faith."[30]

Answers Difficult Questions

The Infinite Way message provides answers to the questions that everyone asks, but few are able to answer. This question is often at the top of the list: "If there is a God, why is there evil in the world?" Joel used the spiritual principles of The Infinite Way to answer that question and other difficult questions that many teachings skirt or avoid.

Ultimate Goal: Benefit the World

Joel knew that realizing the Christhood of our own being is not for our personal benefit, but for the benefit of the world. He taught that every spiritual principle introduced into our consciousness is also introduced into human consciousness at large, and that enlightened individuals can be an influence that

---

29. Recording 526B: 1963 London Work, "The New Message 1963, continued."
30. Recording 225B: 1958 London Closed Class, "Protective Work as It Should Be."

uplifts human consciousness universally. While individual realization is the means, Joel saw the real goal as dispelling the ignorance of truth that blankets human consciousness and is the root of all human troubles.

"Ours is the responsibility to study, to meditate, and to do all that is necessary to bring greater light to our individual consciousness, not for our own sake alone, but that this light which touches our consciousness may flow forth to the world and benefit it, that we may become a center from which goes out this light of healing, regeneration, blessing, peace, comfort, and especially forgiving."[31]

"The vision of The Infinite Way is that, through the spiritual dedication of those who embrace the deepest principles of mystical teaching and reach the heights of the mystical consciousness, human consciousness may be emancipated from itself, that the Presence hidden within may come forth in Its splendor and glory universally."[32]

---

31. *A Parenthesis in Eternity*: Chapter 32, "Address the World Silently with Peace."
32. "The Infinite Way of Life," published in the April 1964 edition of "The Mountain Path Journal," a publication of Sri Ramana Maharshi.

CHAPTER 4

THE NATURE OF GOD

THE NATURE OF GOD is the fundamental principle from which the other principles are derived, so there is an immense amount of material in the books and recordings on the nature of God as it was revealed to Joel. This chapter gives a brief overview of the key aspects of this principle.

CONCEPTS OF GOD

Often when Joel taught about the nature of God, he began by observing that everyone has some concept of God, even if their concept is that there is no God. He invited us to think about where our concepts of God came from:

" Stop and think for a moment where your ideas of God have come from. Who gave them to you? Is it not true that you, yourself, either made up your ideas or concept of God, or you read something and accepted some version of what someone else believed, or you have been taught from infancy to accept someone else's concept of God? Are your ideas of God man-made or are they the result of inner experience?"[1]

---

1. *The Art of Spiritual Healing*: Chapter 2, "Is God a Servant?"

Joel explained that no concept of God is God Itself, and that eventually we must rise above all concepts.

"The hardest part of your spiritual journey is to rise above the concepts of God that you have always accepted. Whether your concept of God has come from a church, from your parents, or from your own experience in life, regardless of where or how you acquired your particular concept of God and regardless of what that concept may be, it is not God. . . . And so, every student must eventually realize that he has to rise above all his concepts of God before he can have an *experience* of God."[2]

Encouraging us to put aside our concepts, Joel suggested that we ask anew, "What is God?"

"It isn't easy, after you have been steeped in centuries of worship and adoration of a false image, to come to a place in consciousness when you can acknowledge it and ask yourself, 'What is God?' . . . If we haven't the courage to acknowledge that what has been given to us in the past four thousand years has not stood up, has not answered, has not functioned, we never will be ready for the next step. We must empty out the vessel of our false beliefs and faiths and images, in order that we may be refilled with truth."[3]

---

2. *The Contemplative Life*: Chapter 2, "Erasing Our Concepts of God, Prayer, and Grace."
3. Recording 547B: 1964 Oahu/Maui Series, "Between Two Worlds—Material Sense, Spiritual Consciousness."

WE CAN LEARN THE NATURE OF GOD

Joel taught that God is an experience, and so we cannot define God or have a correct concept of God. But he acknowledged that we can know the *nature* of God. To know the nature of something is to know the inherent qualities or character of it.

"What is God? That is the problem—*what* is God? Now of course, The Infinite Way doesn't tell you *what* God is. That would be presumptuous. It can only go so far as to tell you the *nature* of God. God Itself must reveal Itself to you. That is an individual experience. No one ever can tell you *what* God is.

"John can say that God is love. I'm sure you know that you don't know what that means. And Jesus can say that God is Father, and I'm sure you know that you don't know what that means, because he certainly didn't mean human father. . . . And the Hindus call God 'Mother,' and you know that they do not mean that in any human sense.

"As you go through the religious literature of the world, you find that there are hundreds and hundreds of men and women who have had the actual experience of God, and each one has told of that experience in one way or another. And yet very few of us, even after reading all that literature, know God or know what God is. The reason is that . . . no one can tell us what God is, except that they can tell us what God is to *them*.

"Now I can tell you, and have told you, many times in the writings what God is to me. That does not necessarily mean that that's what God is, because God has meant many things to me. Since the days of 'Now I lay me down to sleep,' I've gone through many, many concepts of what God is and discarded them one after another . . .

"Now, I can tell you, from my experience, the *nature* of God, but I cannot make that real to you, except in proportion as it becomes real to you through an inner experience. Everything ultimately must come as an activity in your own consciousness. Otherwise, it remains only words—clouds without rain, descriptions, synonyms—but not the *experience* itself. So, we take as the most important part of spiritual living, gaining some degree of awareness of the *nature* of God . . ."[4]

THE NATURE OF GOD

Joel taught that the fundamental nature of God is ONE—one infinite Presence and Power. Yet, he said, there are many facets, or aspects, to that oneness. In the writings and recordings, Joel elaborated on these facets of the nature of God, much as one might explore the facets of a single diamond.

" The synonyms of God do not mean separate qualities of God, but all qualities of one, just as for instance, we may know of one that she is a mother, a wife, a sister, and a daughter. How many of her are there? One. But those titles denote the different parts she plays in life. They denote the different relationships to the world. She can be a mother, a wife, a sister, and a daughter all at the same time and still be only one. And so, God is love, and God is life, and God is law. God is soul. God is the substance of the universe. God is the activity of the universe. Still, it is all God. These different names or

---

4. Recording 70B: 1954 Honolulu Lecture Series, "Nature of God, Prayer, and Error."

synonyms merely define the character or characteristics of God."[5]

Omniscience, Omnipotence, and Omnipresence

Joel put special emphasis on three of the many aspects of the nature of God:

" To understand the nature of God, the three words 'omniscience,' 'omnipotence,' and 'omnipresence' need to be indelibly impressed on consciousness, for without the fullest understanding of their meaning, a student can never approach God."[6]

Omniscience refers to God as the infinite intelligence that maintains and sustains the universe.

" If God is infinite intelligence, He needs no advice, no instructions from you or me, for He is the infinite, all-knowing Consciousness, the Wisdom great enough to form this universe, to maintain it, to sustain it, and to give us the spiritual laws by which we live."[7]

" Suppose that we had to remind God to put apples on apple trees, peaches on peach trees, or berries on berry bushes; or suppose that we had to remind God that we need or do not need so much rain or remind Him every evening that it should become dark, and the stars should come out and the moon. God is doing all these things without our advice or petitions, and can we

---

5. Recording 616A: 1951 First Seattle Series, "The Practitioner of Spiritual Healings."
6. *A Message for the Ages*: Chapter 3, "Now I See."
7. *I Stand on Holy Ground*: Chapter 2, "From Practicing the Presence to the Prayer of Listening."

not trust Him enough to know our needs without reminding Him of them?

"If God knows enough to continue to put the fish in the sea and the birds in the air, if God knows enough to keep the tides in their places, ebbing and flowing on schedule, if God knows enough to keep this earth and all the other planets in their orbits, surely God knows our need, and if God has the love to supply all the needs of this world, God has enough love to supply us with ours."[8]

" The nature of God is infinite intelligence and divine love. Therefore, we never have to tell God anything, advise God, or influence God, because God is already infinite intelligence. We need never ask anything of God because God is divine love and, as the Master has told us, 'It is your Father's good pleasure to give you the kingdom,'[9] not have us ask for it, beg for it, or plead for it."[10]

Omnipotence means that God is the infinite and only power, and that there can be no other power.

" Omnipotence is the next word that must become an integral part of your being. There are few persons in all the world who really believe that God is omnipotent. Not even the composers who have written hymns to an omnipotent God or the ministers who keep talking about the omnipotence of God fifty-two weeks a year believe it. True, they pay lip service to it.

---

8. *The Contemplative Life*: Chapter 6, "Contemplative Meditation."
9. Luke 12:32.
10. *God Formed Us for His Glory*: Chapter 8, "Illumined Prayer."

"But if you spend a few weeks or months with the nature of God as omnipotence and get the realization of it, what will you ever need God-power for after that? Will there be any other power to take to God to be overcome, risen above, or destroyed, if God is omnipotent? If you catch the nature of God as omnipotence, can you ever again ask God to do anything, or even expect it? If God could come down to your level of thought, He might say, 'Well, what is this power that you want Me to do something about? The power of sin, the power of disease, the power of lack? If they are powers, then *I* am not omnipotent, so how do you know *I* am strong enough for the job? But if I am omnipotent, you do not need *My* power, because there is no other power.'"[11]

Omnipresence declares the infinite, all-presence of God, which means that there can be no other presence. That means that we are never outside the presence of God.

"The grace of God and the blessings of God come to us for one reason only and that is that God is omnipresence. God is here where we are, for no reason for which we are responsible. The very nature of God is omnipresence, so we are always in the presence of God, are always being blessed by that presence, and are always receiving the grace of God—not for reason of our own worthiness, only because of God's nature."[12]

---

11. *A Message for the Ages*: Chapter 3, "Now I See."
12. *Showing Forth the Presence of God*: Chapter 3, "God's Blessing Is Not Dependent on Thought or Thing."

"Anyone that ever catches the significance of omni-presence is automatically freed from fear of any nature, and the reason is this: The only reason any of us has to fear is if we are not in God's presence, because then that puts the deal up to us. What can I do about this? And if I am not sufficient, I am doomed. Right? Whether it is being on a battlefront, or being in a city that has contagion or epidemic, what can you do about it if it is just you there alone? On the other hand, what can any of these beliefs do if God is there with you? . . .

"Telling you once that God is omnipresence, and that God is present where you are, may be teaching it to you, but that is no guarantee that you are learning it. Only when it is drilled into your consciousness day after day, week after week, month after month, will something inside of you explode and you will exclaim, 'Oh, God is here!' Or you will hear inside of you, 'I will never leave you, nor forsake you.'[13] . . . What more could you possibly want than the assurance of God's presence?"[14]

Summarizing these three aspects of the nature of God, Joel said:

"Individually we can turn and ask ourselves questions about the nature of God: What do I suppose God to be? Do I think of God as a great power fighting other powers? If I do, then I deny omnipotence, because under omnipotence, God must be all-power, and there can be no other powers for God to fight. Do I accept the presence of evil in a person or in a condition? Then I am

---

13. Hebrews 13:5.
14. Recording 509A: 1963 Instructions for Teaching The Infinite Way, "Nature of God, Error, Prayer—for Six Lessons."

denying omnipresence, because omnipresence means the all-presence of God, and if there is an all-presence of God, there can be no other presence: no evil presence, no negative presence. Do I believe that anyone on earth can tell God what I need? If I do, then I am denying omniscience, the all-wisdom of God who knows our need before we ask."[15]

While Joel emphasized omniscience, omnipotence, and omnipresence, The Infinite Way message is rich with explorations of many other aspects of the nature of God: God is Life; God is Love; God is Law; God is the creating, maintaining, and sustaining principle of all that is; God does not punish or reward, give or withhold. As Joel presented these aspects of the nature of God, he pointed out that accepting these and living in conscious awareness of them can change our experience dramatically.

God Is Life

"God is life, infinite life; and therefore, God must be the life of man. That life which is God cannot be diseased. God, the life of man, cannot be weak; God, the life of man, cannot be old; God, the life of man, is infinite, immortal, and eternal."[16]

"Now then, this correct letter of truth will reveal to you that since God is one, and since God is life, that there is only one life. Now, affirming that is almost as useless as thinking it. But to *know* that God is the one and only life immediately stops your fearing for

---

15. *The Journey Back to the Father's House*: Chapter 9, "The Spiritual Kingdom Made Tangible."
16. *The Heart of Mysticism: Volume 5, The 1958 Infinite Way Letters*: Chapter 11: November, "The Fruits of the Spirit."

your life, whether you shall lose it, or whether you shall gain it, whether your life be thirty years of age or ninety years of age. You can have no fear for it as long as you know that there is but one God, and that one God is life. Therefore, there is but one life, and that life never had a beginning and will never have an ending. But you must *know* this correct letter in order to gain the conviction that leads to the spirit or consciousness of truth."[17]

Can you see how a realization of that aspect of the nature of God—that God is the one life—could change your experience?

God Is Love

Love is another facet of the nature of God that can transform our lives.

" Can we accept the fact that *God is love*, not God is love *if* we behave in a certain way, or not just when we are worthy and deserving? . . . The principle is this: Since *God is love*, our good must be infinite without any ifs, ands, or buts, because God's grace is not dependent upon something that you or I do or do not do. The grace of God cannot be withheld. We can turn the electricity on or off and we can turn the water on or off, but we cannot start or stop the flow of God. *God is, and God is love* in Its completeness and fullness."[18]

" It will not be difficult to live, and move, and have our being in the God that Christ Jesus set forth for mankind, because this God is a God of love. This God

---

17. Recording 150A: 1956 Second Steinway Hall Closed Class, "God Is One—One Power—One Life—One, One, One."
18. *Living The Infinite Way*: Chapter 6, "I Am the Vine."

evidences His love, not in punishing us, killing us, or ordering our execution; this God shows Itself forth as love by forgiving seventy times seven; by asking everyone even to pray for those of us who have been persecutors or in some other way devils on earth.

"God proves to be a God of love by the ministry It sent forth through Christ Jesus. 'I seek not mine own will, but the will of the Father which hath sent me.'[19] The will of the Father that Jesus sets forth is: 'Heal the sick, cleanse the lepers, raise the dead, cast out devils: freely ye have received, freely give'[20]—not murder people, not 'call them home' with disease and accidents, not inflict punishment such as being stoned to death, or the age-old law of 'an eye for an eye and a tooth for a tooth.' The God Jesus taught is love, but this God evidences that love through healing, through forgiving, even unto seventy times seven, those who are instruments for evil in any and every form."[21]

God Is Law

Knowing the nature of God as law can alter our perceptions, too.

"Now another facet of God is that God is Law. Everything that functions in the kingdom of God functions under divine law. Whether it is mathematics or music, whether it is art or literature, whether it is the sun, moon, and stars—everything that has emanated, everything that is an expression of the consciousness of God, is under spiritual law. Therefore, in our under-

---

19. John 5:30.
20. Matthew 10:8.
21. *The Journey Back to the Father's House*: Chapter 10, "God's Dominion, Not Man's Domination."

standing of the nature of God, we . . . have to see the lawfulness of God."[22]

"Let us take the word 'law.' God is law. . . . You never need anything but that one statement. Why? Well, if God is law, and God is infinite, law must be infinite. It's God's law that is infinite. Well then, is there a law of sin? Is there a law of disease? Is there a law of limitation? Is there a law of climate? Is there a law of weather? Is there a law of foods? Is there a law of medicines? Why, no. Have we just said that God is law? That leaves only one law in this world, and that law must be God's law. That law must be good law.

"Now, tell me, what are we doing sitting around studying? . . . Ah! I'll tell you the answer. There isn't one of us who believes it! There isn't one of us here who can accept it! It's too deep; it's too far. The mind won't grasp it, and only as you come into spiritual consciousness can you grasp . . . that tremendous fact that God's law is the only law. Then in that instant, you could really raise the dead, but it's only five minutes later that you're believing in a law of climate, or a law of heredity, or a law of vitamins, or a law of foods, or a law of something else. It isn't your fault. This isn't a criticism or condemnation, and certainly it isn't judgment, because I'm right in the same seat with you on that. I have wonderful moments when God's law is the only law and I see beautiful things from it, and then some other law comes to plague me fifteen minutes later. . . .

"Now then, the secret is that God is law, but that God is the *only* law, because God is infinite. And

---

22. *Spiritual Power of Truth*: Chapter 9, "God and Error."

since God is also good, self-created, self-maintained, self-sustained, this law of God is self-maintained and self-sustained and is eternal and infinite and omnipresent. So, any other law—law of heredity, law of limitation, law of disease, infection, contagion—these are not laws, but illusions."[23]

God Is the Creative, Maintaining and Sustaining Principle

" G od is the creative principle and power, the maintaining and sustaining influence of this universe. God is being God all of the time, and He is being God without direction or petition on our part, and without affirmation or prayer of any nature."[24]

In one of his classes,[25] Joel gives a beautiful explanation of the nature of God as the creative, maintaining, and sustaining principle. He points out that there is only one power, not in the sense that it does anything to anything, but in the sense of its being a creative, sustaining, and maintaining power. Joel reminds us that as we observe nature, we can see laws operating, such as the law of like begetting like. If you plant tomato seeds, you will always get tomatoes. Blueberries always come from blueberry bushes and apples from apple trees. What brought that law of like begetting like into existence? What made the ocean salty, or put birds in the air and fish in the sea? What did that?

As Joel says, we can call it by many names, but never was it a human being. We can call it a "creative principle," and since those things have been going on for ages, we can also call it a

23. Recording 60A: 1954 Chicago Practitioner Class, "Nature of Error."
24. *The Heart of Mysticism: Volume 2, The 1955 Infinite Way Letters*: Chapter 7: July, "Meditation for Beginners."
25. Recording 175A: 1956 New York Laurelton Hotel Closed Class, "I Say unto You."

"maintaining and sustaining principle." Further, Joel says, whatever it is that creates, also maintains and sustains, and nothing has ever interfered with it. No person has stopped the earth from spinning, or made roses come from tomato seeds, or stopped birds from flying, or changed the tide tables or the phases of the moon.

"The nature of God is such that what God is not already doing, God cannot do and could not be induced to do. Understand that clearly. What God is not doing now, it would be a waste of time asking or expecting Him to do: No one prays to God for the sun to rise in the morning or to set at night; no one prays to God to arrange the incoming and outgoing tides; no one prays to God to have roses come from roses, or pineapples from pineapples, or butter from milk; no one prays to God to change the laws of automotive engineering or airplane dynamics. In short, most people seem perfectly willing to let God run His own universe in His own way until their own little selves become involved. Then they turn to God and say, 'O God, won't you do this for me? Won't you protect me or mine? Won't you heal me or mine? Won't you send food and clothing to me and mine?'"[26]

If we can see that God as creative principle brought us forth as well, why would we ever think that we were exceptions to the perpetual maintaining and sustaining activity of God? Why would we think that God maintains and sustains everything else, but that we must fend for ourselves? Do you see how realizing the nature of God as the creative, maintaining, and sustaining power could change your outlook on life?

---

26. *The Art of Spiritual Healing*: Chapter 2, "Is God a Servant?"

Joel said that when you turn to God, it is like turning on the television. Turning on the television does not *create* the program. You tune in to a program that is *already* in progress. The creative, maintaining, and sustaining activity of God is going on eternally now, and all you need to do is tune in and behold.

God Does Not Punish or Reward, Give or Withhold

One of the most tenacious erroneous concepts of God is that God can punish and reward, or give and withhold. Joel said that if we are under that belief, it is difficult to find harmony in our lives because we will always seek to be good so that God will reward us, and to give up our sins so that God will not punish us. But Joel was quick to point out, "God has no interest in your goodness and will not reward it, and God has no interest in your sins and will not punish them."[27]

" I t is dangerous to accept the belief of a God that punishes and rewards. God does not punish, and God does not reward. Whatever God does, God merely does as a function of God. You might liken it to the sun and sunlight. The sun does not shine and give light and warmth as a reward to anybody for anything. To shine is its function, and it cannot withhold sunshine, not even from the sinner. God is not a human being. God does not act like a human parent or a judge on the bench. Not at all! God is infinite being and is forever being infinite being. God cannot give and God cannot withhold. God can only *be*."[28]

---

27. *Beyond Words and Thoughts*: Chapter 1, "Toward the Experience."
28. *The Art of Spiritual Living*: Chapter 8, "The Fruitage of Knowing God Aright."

" It may be that you believe that you have problems because you deserve them; because you've sinned—an act of omission or commission—that you've wandered away from God. Well, you're going to have to get over that in a hurry, because God does not punish, ever, under any circumstance. There isn't anybody in the world who has ever been under the condemnation of God; and nobody has ever been punished by God. The belief that God punishes man is one of the errors that has kept man from living in God's embrace."[29]

Does that mean that sin is not punished? No, but God is not involved in the punishment.

" God never rewards virtue. God never punishes sin. True, sin is punished—by the sin. In other words, the person who makes the wrong electrical connection will be burned, but he cannot blame the electricity for this. The electricity did not punish him: He brought about his own punishment by his incorrect act. The person who goes into the water, becomes frightened, flounders around, and finally almost drowns, cannot blame the water, but rather, his ignorance of how to behave in the water. No one can violate law and not be punished for such violation; but no one should blame God for the ensuing punishment. The fault lies not in God but in individual conduct and in individual misperception of the nature of the law."[30]

Just as God does not punish or reward, God neither withholds nor gives. God IS.

---

29. Recording 380B: 1960 Christchurch Closed Class, "The Next Principles."
30. *The Thunder of Silence*: Chapter 2, "Karmic Law."

"God is not a withholding God, neither is He a giving God. God never gives nor bestows anything! . . . God is Love. God is *being* Love. God is Life. God is *being* Life. God is not withholding life, nor is God going to bestow life, since God, Itself, *is* Life . . . If God were waiting for you to be good or deserving, or to find the right form of prayer or method of treatment, He would be a cruel and severe God indeed. God has nothing to give, and God will never give more than He is giving you now!"[31]

"It is not the nature of God to withhold from you and then give you those very things because you pray for them or because you have been good. That is the Santa Claus concept of God. As long as you entertain such a concept of God, . . . you have no hope whatsoever of knowing God aright. The more you realize that God is not a rewarding God or a punishing God, but that the nature of God is Infinite Love and Infinite Wisdom, the clearer you will see that there is no need to tell God of your needs or to ask Him to fulfill them. Doing so is going back to the pagan belief that God has been withholding from you. It is not in His consciousness to withhold anything from you or to punish you for anything."[32]

Then why don't we always experience the beneficence of God?

"If God is love, God is not withholding, and . . . if God is Infinite Intelligence, God does not have to be enlightened as to our needs. When we begin to perceive

---

31. *The Heart of Mysticism: Volume 2, The 1955 Infinite Way Letters*: Chapter 6: June, "Higher Views of God, Prayer and the Self."
32. *Invisible Supply*: Chapter 4, "Overcoming Our Sense of Separation from God."

this, we begin to wonder then, *why*? Why are the harmonies absent from our lives? Why is health so difficult to attain? Why is supply such a difficult subject for the mass of mankind? Why are harmonious human relationships so difficult to attain, and to maintain? . . .

"If I am not receiving God's grace, it has *nothing whatsoever* to do with God! It has to do with *me* and my ignorance [of truth], which can be corrected because God's rain falls on the just and the unjust. God's grace is my sufficiency, and where the Spirit of the Lord is, there is freedom, liberty. Where is the Spirit of the Lord, if not omnipresent, if not here where we are? Therefore, here where we are . . . the Presence of God is, and is available, and needs only acknowledgment.

"'Acknowledge Him in all thy ways; lean not onto thine own understanding.'[33] . . . Are we acknowledging [Him] in all our ways? If not, there has arisen the *sense* of separation, which cheats us of this grace of God, which is at hand. God is not withholding, but neither is God giving. God is not giving anything to anyone at any time. God is *being*. God is infinite being. God is omniscience, omnipotence, omnipresence. God is all-being, here and now, and God is being God all of the time. So there is no withholding, and there is no giving. There is just *being*, and our acknowledgment of that brings it into our experience."[34]

God Is Not Personal

Another facet of the nature of God is that God is not "personal," in the sense that the activity of God is not directed to specific persons. Just as the sun shines universally and anyone can enjoy

---

33. Proverbs 3:5-6.
34. Recording 286A: 1959 New York Open Class, "The Nature of God and Prayer."

its benefits, the love of God and the activity of God are eternally beaming forth and cannot be directed to a specific person.

"Do you see why the God-experience can come only when you have relaxed your personal efforts . . . and come to the realization that there is nothing personal about the activity of God in the sense that God would do any more for me than He would do for you? Never believe that God did more for Jesus Christ than He would do for you or for me. There is no such God!

"God is not a superperson who goes around saying, 'I will do this for this you here, but I will not do it for that you over there.' . . . There are no exceptions in the laws of God. It can make no difference to God whether a person is white or black, Jew or Gentile, bond or free, saint or sinner. It can make no difference whatsoever!"[35]

Further, Joel taught that God is not "personal" in the sense that God is not a personal being "out there" separate and apart from your own being.

"As long as you believe there is a God out there separate and apart from your being, just so long do you personalize God and set up the picture of an entity, identity, or a being outside of you. God is being, but not a being. God is being you and being me. So to set up a God separate from that being produces the sense of separation that keeps us in ignorance."[36]

"For thousands of years God has been considered as something separate and apart from us. Today, how-

---

35. *Beyond Words and Thoughts*: Chapter 1, Toward the Experience."
36. *The Mystical I*: Chapter 6, "Impersonalizing God."

ever, we are no longer willing to accept a far-off God, because we have come to understand that God is the Soul of our being; God is the Mind, the Spirit, the very Substance of which we are formed. God is the center of our being. God is the infinite consciousness of our being."[37]

This aspect of the nature of God—that God is manifest as our very own being—is the province of the next chapter, "The Nature of Individual Being."

God Does Not Function in the Human Scene

The Infinite Way message is full of surprises to those who have known only an orthodox teaching. Many aspects of the message stand in stark contrast to orthodox teachings, and yet we may feel the rightness of them. Sometimes these provocative, unorthodox ideas turn out to be what inspires our interest in exploring The Infinite Way: "Whatever does Joel mean by *that?* Could it be true?"

The teaching that God does not function in the human scene may be one of those surprises for you. In this introductory book, we only skim the surface of this topic, but Joel addresses this theme in depth in many books and recordings.

When Joel tells the story of his own spiritual journey, he says that it began with the realization that there is no God in the human world.

" The Infinite Way came into being when I realized that there is no God in the human world. If there were a God in the human world, rape, arson, murder, wars, dens of iniquity, drug addiction, and all the other afflictions of mankind would be impossible. Not one

---

37. *The Master Speaks*: Chapter 2, "Reality of Spirit."

of these evidences of man's inhumanity to man could occur in the presence of God. Everything that is taking place in this world of ours is taking place only because there is no God in the human scene.

"This was the original unfoldment that was given to me some time after 1909, and this is what started me on the search. I have never doubted that there is a God, but now at least I know that there is no God in 'this world,' and I know now, too, that all the going to church and all the praying are not going to bring one here. People have been going to church to pray since before the days of the ancient Hebrews and have done so continuously ever since. They have prayed every kind of prayer that has ever been known, and still the world keeps right on falling apart.

"Thus the search began: Where is God? What is God? How do we bring God into our experience?"[38]

When a human tragedy occurs, often we see the clerics and spiritual teachers of the world on television or social media, trying to answer the question, "Why does God allow such things?" Many of these people accept the premise of the question, namely that God is directing the affairs of mankind and has the choice to allow tragedy or not. Then, reasoning from that mistaken assumption, some say that God allows evil so He can draw good out of it. Others say that God's ways are not our ways, and so we cannot understand why He allows it. The more extreme say that God is punishing us. Joel's answer is quite different.

"Let me pose this question to you: 'Can you possibly believe that if we were under the law of God, that if mankind actually was God-maintained and

---

38. *Beyond Words and Thoughts*: Chapter 1: "Toward the Experience."

God-sustained, that there would be rape, arson, murder, war? Can you actually believe that such things come under the reign of God? . . . Would there be a death if man were God-governed? Would there be a disease? Would there be these human horrors that we read of in the paper every day indicating man's inhumanity to man, if God were governing the scene? Of course not! God is not in the whirlwind; God is not in sin; God is not in disease or death.

"The tragedy is—and it happened only last week—a minster reading a funeral service. Over half a dozen people had been killed in an accident, and he said, 'We must take consolation from the fact that God giveth and God taketh away.' Can you believe that God sent an airplane hurtling out of the sky to kill the people in it? Well, I cannot, and I will not. It is not my idea of God—not at all."[39]

Joel had the realization that such things happen, not because God caused or allowed them, but because God does not function in the human scene.

"God does not function in the human scene. If God functioned in the human scene, there would not be a sin, a disease, or a death. There would not be a hospital or a mental institution if God were in the scene. The omnipotence, the omnipresence, and the omniscience of God preclude the possibility of any form of discord being present.

"Human life is not under God guidance. When we rise above the human scene and our consciousness expands to an acceptance, a receptivity, and a respon-

---

39. Recording 487A: 1962 London Closed Class, "Being Unclothed and Clothed Upon."

siveness to the activity of God, then we are no longer human beings: we are the sons of God, spiritually fed, spiritually housed, spiritually clothed, spiritually governed. 'I live; yet not I, but Christ liveth in me'[40]—but not as a human being. If Christ were living the life of human beings, they would certainly not be bombed out of any place, nor would they be in sin or discord of any nature. Where God is in operation, there is harmony."[41]

In other words, God does not operate in the human scene, in human consciousness, and further, God has no awareness of the human scene. Joel taught that when we experience human discords and tragedies, we are outside the jurisdiction, law, and grace of God, and the question is, "How do we return?" The return comes when we *realize* the omnipresence and omnipotence of God—when we *realize* it, not just know about it or believe in it. So, The Infinite Way message does not focus on trying to bring God into the human scene, but on awakening to and realizing Christhood, rising into the higher dimensions of spiritual consciousness, where perfect harmony already eternally IS and can be revealed.

REPRISE: GOD IS AN EXPERIENCE

These quotations from Joel give a taste of his teaching about the nature of God. As was said in Chapter 2, The Infinite Way is a spiritual path that begins with a teaching, becomes a way of life, and culminates in an experience. That experience is the experience of God.

---

40. Galatians 2:20.
41. *God Formed Us for His Glory*: Chapter 3, "The Nature of the Messiah."

God is an experience, but understanding and contemplating the nature of God and living to the best of our ability in accord with these revelations prepares us for that experience.

" G od cannot be known with the mind or thought processes. What is known of God through the mind is but the concept of God—an ever-changing concept— even though God Itself is changeless. Yet the ability to intellectually ponder these concepts leads inevitably to the higher consciousness where God is first discerned, then realized."[42]

---

42. *The Heart of Mysticism: Volume 1, The 1954 Infinite Way Letters*: Chapter 11: November, "Attain That Mind."

CHAPTER 5

THE NATURE OF
INDIVIDUAL BEING

THE SECOND OF the four fundamental principles of The Infinite Way is the nature of individual being. Joel taught that God is manifest as individual being, which means that the true nature of individual being is the nature of God.

" The Infinite Way [teaches] the nature of God *as* individual being, which means God *as* your being. Unless we catch this idea of oneness, we miss this basic spiritual premise—that there are not both God *and* you. The only way we can realize oneness is to understand God *as* you . . . The life which is God is your individual life; therefore, your life is just as immortal as the life we call God."[1]

The nature of individual being comes from the nature of God as Omnipresence: As Joel said, "Because of Omnipresence, God constitutes individual being."[2]

---

1. *The Master Speaks*: Chapter 18, "The Infinite Way."
2. *Consciousness Is What I Am*: Chapter 10, "The Consciousness of Truth is the Healer."

"Omnipresence, of course, refers to the all-presence of God, but since the kingdom of God is within you, Omnipresence is right where you are. . . . Omnipresence is an 'already' fact. In other words, the presence of God is *already* where I am. 'The place whereon thou standest is holy ground'[3] because God is there. Therefore, Omnipresence is *already* the established fact, and the only reason why you may know sin, disease, lack, limitation, accident, is not because of any absence of Omnipresence, but because of the lack of *realization* of Omnipresence. Omnipresence is where you are; that is, the presence of God and the Spirit of God is where you are, but it takes your *realization* of this to make it a living factor in your experience."[4]

God is expressed *as* individual being—as your individual being, your true identity, and *as* the true identity of every individual. "You are not separate and apart from God: you are in and of God, and God is in and of you."[5] In other words, there is only one Presence, so if you are present, you are that Presence.

"Everything you know starts with the nature of God, but if you were to concern yourself only with the nature of God, you'll be concerned with something that at least in belief you would be setting aside from yourself, separate and apart from your own being. So whenever you think of the nature of God, think of the nature of God as the nature of individual being. Then you will be able to understand that whatever you find God to be,

---

3. Exodus 3:5.
4. Recording 533B: 1963 Manchester Work, "Spiritual Discernment, Through Meditation, Reveals the Kingdom of God."
5. *A Message for the Ages:* Chapter 7, "Material Sense of Demonstration or the Unfoldment of Grace."

that is what you must find your self to be and the self of your patient or friend or relative.

"This is important. There are too many people who know God as mind, life, truth, love, and so forth, but do not realize that when they are speaking of God—of mind, life, truth, love, spirit, law—they are likewise speaking of their own individual being, since 'I and the Father are one.'[6]

"So, remember that you must above all things know the nature of God, and because you know the nature of God, you must know that that is the nature of individual being. This realization of oneness, of unity, is more important than you might believe at this moment because without it, you will be trying in some way to bring this nature of God to the individual instead of realizing it *as* the very nature of individual being. "[7]

THE HUMAN BEING IS NOT THE MANIFESTATION OF GOD

In teaching the nature of individual being, Joel explains that there *seem* to be two of us: our inner self and our outer self, or our humanhood and our Godhood.

" N ow there are two of us: there is the man of earth that we are as human beings, and there is the man who has his being in Christ, which is our true identity."[8]

When Joel says that God is manifest *as* you, he is *not* saying that God is manifest as your *humanhood,* your personality, the

---

6. John 10:30.
7. Recording 26A: 1953 Second Hawaiian Series, "The Four Essentials of Healing."
8. *Spiritual Power of Truth*: Chapter 5, "Universal Hypnotism."

"outer I," or human ego. God is manifest as the "inner *I*" of you; the essential, spiritual, divine being that you truly are, have always been, and always will be.

"It isn't true that the kingdom of God is within a *human* being. If it were, a human being would never need anything. It isn't true that God's life is a human being's life, or a human being wouldn't be sick, sinful, or die. You see, all of this spiritual truth is true about your *spiritual identity*, the Son of God, which is your true being, but from which, as human beings, we have a *sense* of separation."[9]

"Again we come to that word 'I' and the two ways of using it. There is the I that refers to our humanhood. That is the I that has problems and is always overcoming something. But there is that other *I* which has never had a problem, which was never born, and which will never die. It is the *I* that I am, the *I* that constitutes our spiritual identity that is under the law of God. It is the *I* that we spiritually are which lives by grace."[10]

"Sometimes students write, 'I've realized that I am God.' But that could not be true. We can say, 'God is my being; God constitutes my being;' but to turn around and say that we constitute God's being is a little bit far-fetched. If we understood the word *I* correctly, that would be different. But if we did, we would never make the statement, 'I am God.'

"The statement 'I am God,' cannot be voiced: it can only be heard. When the voice announces within us, 'Be

---

9. Recording 52A: 1953 First New York Closed Class, "The Human and the Spiritual."
10. *The Mystical I:* Chapter 9, "The Temple Not Made with Hands."

still and know that I am God,"[11] that verily is God. But the moment we say, 'I am God,' that cannot be, unless we are referring to the mystical I. We need to be watchful lest we attempt to make a human being God . . ."[12]

DISPELLING ERRONEOUS CONCEPTS OF OURSELVES

Just as we may have mistaken concepts of God, we may also have erroneous concepts of ourselves. We may believe that we are human, limited, mortal, sick, sinning, ignorant, or in lack. As we release and dispel these mistaken concepts, we make room for the truth about individual being.

"Mystical wisdom does not teach that a mortal is to become immortal, but that he must 'die daily' and be reborn of the Spirit; that is, he must *awaken* to the awareness of his true identity, and just as he would drop any illusion, so he must drop once and for all time the belief that he is fallen man.

"When we are unclothed of mortality and clothed with immortality, there is no fallen man; there is only the original, perfect man, the spiritual identity which is now and always has been, intact, just as a child taken from a family of wealth and culture and brought up in poverty, possibly in sin, disease, and ignorance, is still the child with the same identity and potentiality with which he was originally born. He has merely been clothed upon with an illusory identity, but his name, identity, wealth, and all the other things that belonged to him at birth could be restored in any moment. This child did not fall:

---

11. Psalm 46:10.
12. *Spiritual Discernment*: Chapter 2, "God Must Be an Experience, Not a Concept."

he is the same child he was at birth. All the experiences that he has gone through have merely been imposed upon him, but his original heritage and identity are what they were in the beginning."[13]

When we first learn the truth of our identity, it can seem too enormous to grasp and too fantastic to believe. Our *human* experience does not bear it out. We hear that in our spiritual identity, we are infinite, yet we might entertain a sense of lack or limitation. We hear that we are eternal and immortal, yet we may have a sense of mortality. We hear that we are omniscient, yet we may experience a sense of ignorance. We hear that we are omnipotent, yet we might feel a sense of fear. This is because we have not fully *realized* the truth of our being. The Infinite Way teaches that it is possible for any individual with sufficient commitment and dedication to fully experience their true identity and to live by it, thereby dispelling any sense of limitation, mortality, ignorance, or fear.

" You are not separate and apart from God and, through this work, going to get back to God. Through this work, you are going to awaken out of the dream that there can be any separation. If you have been dreaming you are drowning in the ocean, awakening does not take the water away from you; and it does not take you out of the ocean. It reveals to you that you are in bed. So this work never takes you out of sin, disease, or lack. It wakes you up, and then you look around and realize you are in heaven. You have been there all the time, dreaming you were in hell."[14]

---

13. *A Parenthesis in Eternity*: Chapter 12, "The Discovery of the Self."
14. *Awakening Mystical Consciousness*: Chapter 7, "Concepts or Is?"

THE CHRIST

This presence of God in us, or *as* us, is also known as "the Christ." Remember that when Joel uses the term "Christ," he is *not* referring to Jesus. He is referring to the divine Presence within every individual, the true Self, the pure and complete manifestation of God, the spirit of God in man. This indwelling Presence has been known by many names—Krishna, Buddha, Immanuel, and Messiah, among others.

" There is something called the Christ. The Christ is not just a name given to some intangible or nebulous thing. The Christ is a divine reality that is a living presence, and it is omnipresent. It is right where you are and right where I am. Christ is not a person. Christ is a principle. It is a principle of life. It is a principle of God, which forms the reality of your being. . . . We have become, in belief, separated from the very Christ of our being. It is much the same as if we lived in a house with the blinds drawn and had become accustomed to walking around in darkness, semi-darkness, or in a room artificially lighted. As time passed, we actually forgot that there was such a thing as sunshine and that outside our drawn shades was the bright, warm sun. In our humanhood we have done just that. We have had the blinds drawn—our mental blinds. This is what Jesus meant when he said, 'Having eyes, see ye not? and having ears, hear ye not?'[15] Those spiritual faculties have been closed, so that we are not aware of the fact that just beyond the range of our humanhood there is the divinity of our being called the Christ, the Spirit of God in man."[16]

---

15. Mark 8:18.
16. *The Master Speaks:* Chapter 14: "Christ Consciousness."

"Ultimately, we shall all discover that our true identity is Christ, and although we may have been brought up as Jones, Brown, or Smith, our real name—our identity and potentiality—is Christ, the spiritual offspring of God. In the moment that this truth is revealed to us, all that has been imposed upon us by human belief will drop away, and as soon as we begin to perceive our true nature and identity, it will not take long to become accustomed to the atmosphere of Spirit which is our original abiding place."[17]

"The Christ is not visible to the eyes, nor is It audible to the ears; the Christ cannot be touched with the fingers, nor smelled or tasted: The Christ is really a state of divine consciousness which you and I are. It is an incorporeality. In our true state of being, that is what we really are, although that is not what we appear to be to one another. Looking out through the eyes, we behold a finite, limited, and material concept of that which actually is."[18]

The Christ that was manifest as Jesus is the very same Christ that is manifest as your true identity and as the *true* identity of every individual. This divine nature is not apparent in some individuals because they live in ignorance of this truth, and their behavior reflects that ignorance. Nonetheless, Joel re-revealed that Christhood is the essential nature of every individual, and he taught that we can fully experience our Christhood and live by It. When we awaken from the limited human state of con-

17. *A Parenthesis in Eternity*: Chapter 12, "The Discovery of the Self."
18. *The Heart of Mysticism: Volume 6, The 1959 Infinite Way Letters*: Chapter 10: October, "Freeing Ourselves from Universal Claims."

sciousness, which is simply the ignorance of our true nature, we stand revealed as the Christ of being.

"There is within every person the Christ-Self, the real Self, the *I*. On the spiritual path, the goal is the attaining of conscious union with that Self, or the attaining of the realization of the Christ as our identity. This requires a 'dying daily' to the human part of us, the outer part, and being reborn as this true identity; dying to the limited sense of self and being reborn into or as our perfected Self, the Christ-Self. . . .

"Within each of us is the perfect Self that has never fallen, has never left heaven, and therefore can never gain heaven. It is already a state of heaven; it is already living the perfected life, the spiritual life, the Christ-life that can never be crucified, can never be resurrected, cannot ever be ascended. It already is the perfect Self, the son of God, or the Christ within us. It has been called 'the hidden manna,' 'the pearl of great price,' the robe of immortality."[19]

Not only must we learn to know ourselves as the Christ, but we must see others in the same light.

"In order to see anyone correctly, we must develop the habit of looking into his eyes, and then, if we are able to penetrate the depths that lie way, way back of his eyes, we shall see the person in his true identity, behold the reality of his being, and discover that names are but masks for characters in God-consciousness, God-consciousness Itself produced as form. Behind the

---

19. *The Mystical I*: Chapter 9, "The Temple Not Made with Hands."

mask called Bill, James, or Joseph, there is but the one name, G-o-d. . . .

"Then, every time we go to the butcher or the baker, do business with a broker or a banker, enter our home or church, or go to our business, we shall be seeing the Christ-man, a *person without qualities*, a person who, we know within ourselves, has the Soul of God, the mind of God, and the Spirit of God."[20]

" We must acknowledge God as the individual being of even our enemies. . . . There can be only one way to pray for our enemies, and that is to recognize God as their individual being."[21]

GOD IS NOT IN; GOD APPEARS AS

Joel clarified that God is not "in" man, in the sense of two things, one inside the other, but that God appears *as* individual being.

" When Jesus spoke of 'the Father within me,' he was not making of himself some kind of a hollow tube in which God was located. He did not mean that statement in a literal sense. It was his way of referring to God *as* his consciousness, God *as* his being, God *as* his life; but not God *in* his life, not God *in* his body, not even God *in* his mind."[22]

An analogy can be helpful. Gold can be formed into a bracelet, a coin, a goblet, or an electronic component. Each of these forms has a different purpose. The bracelet beautifies, the coin

---

20. *The Thunder of Silence*: Chapter 16, "That Ye May Be the Children of Your Father."
21. *Living by Grace*: Chapter 6, "The Infinite Way Concept of God."
22. *The Master Speaks*: Chapter 17, "The Ever-Present Christ."

is a medium of exchange, the goblet is an instrument for drinking, and the electronic component facilitates computing processes. Yet in its "goldness," each form has all the properties and character of gold. It does not tarnish; it is malleable; it has the same specific weight, density, atomic mass, boiling point, and melting point as the gold of which it is formed.

Neither the bracelet, the coin, the goblet, or the electronic component has to *do* anything to *be* gold; they already *are* gold. Even though their forms differ, and they seem to be separated in time and space, they are the same in *substance*. The gold is not *in* the bracelet, coin, goblet, or electronic component. The gold is formed *as* those things. The gold itself is never personalized or finitized by the form that it takes. In other words, it does not cease to be gold when it is formed. The form is a concept. You could melt down the object, doing away with its form, but you would be left with the same substance, gold.

So with us. God, or spiritual substance, appears to us, or is perceived as, different forms, or individual beings. But God is the substance of each one. The nature and character of God is the same true nature and character for each individual form.

Joel told an ancient story to make the point that God appears *as* individual being.

" A student went to his master in India and said, 'Oh Master, when are you going to reveal God to me?' 'Oh,' the Master said, 'in due time, in due time.' Every day the student came eagerly, 'When am I to know God? When are you to reveal God to me?' Finally, the day came. The Master said, 'This is the day,' and he took him to a temple, and he said, 'I am taking you to this door which you will enter. But I'll tell you that you'll be in one room, but there are three. But you'll have to work your way from the first room into the second, the second into the third. How you'll do it, I don't know, because I don't think there are any exits or entrances.'

"And so he turned the student loose in this first room. And when the student got accustomed to the darkness, he saw that there was a figure of God—Buddha perhaps—in solid gold. It was beautiful. But as he looked at it for a while, the thought came to him, 'No, no, no. This isn't right. There's something wrong here. This isn't right. There's too much heaviness in the air. This isn't right. I must go further.' And so he sought for the entrance to the second room, and we're told that in the course of time he found it, and as he got into the second room, he again became aware of a figure, and this time it was a figure of the Buddha in crystal. 'Ah, now! Now I'm commencing to understand God. Now I'm commencing to know.' But soon he realized, 'This isn't it either. No, no. This isn't it.' And so, he started his search for the third room and eventually reached there. To his surprise, when he got into the third room, he found himself all alone. That was his master's way of revealing God to him." [23]

There is a similar story in the Hebrew tradition, and in that version, when the student came to this third room, he found himself alone with a mirror.

WE ENTERTAIN A *SENSE* OF SEPARATION

The obvious question is, "If all this is true, and my true nature, the essence of my being, is divine, why don't I experience it?" Joel answers this question.

---

23. Recording 123A: 1955 Kailua Study Group, "No Truth Is Truth Except the Truth That Reveals Itself in You."

"The missing link is that in some way or another there is either a separation between me and the God who fills my very being, or else if there isn't an actual separation, I am entertaining a *sense* of separation from that infinity of good.

"Now, of course, there can be no separation, since the relationship was established in the beginning that I and the Father are one. . . . The infinity of God and the infinity of all good is manifest right here as my very being, so that if I am not showing it forth, it isn't because it isn't here; it is because I somewhere have lost that sense of this infinite Presence and am entertaining a *sense* of separation."[24]

"In reality we have never been separated from God; we have never been separated from our good, from our wholeness and completeness; but from the time we were infants, we have been taught about a personal 'I,' and we have, therefore, entertained this false *sense* of self which claims, 'I am Mary,' 'I am Bill,' or 'I am Joel,' instead of humbly realizing: 'Be still and know that I am God.'[25] *I at the center of me is God, and therefore, I live by Grace and by divine inheritance.*"[26]

How do we dispel this *sense* of separation and experience the truth of individual being?

"You will not solve all your problems by an intellectual agreement that *I* is God, that *I* is infinite, and therefore, that *I* is infinite wealth and infinite health.

---

24. Recording 625B: 1954 New York Lecture Series, "The Missing Link."
25. Psalm 46:10.
26. *A Parenthesis in Eternity*: Chapter 16, "The Secret of the Word Made Flesh."

Ultimately, that truth will solve all your problems, but not until it has been rooted and grounded in your individual consciousness."[27]

In other words, not only must we understand and accept the truth of Oneness; we must *realize* it, in the sense that it must become *real* to us.

This *I* of your being is not something other than your Self or something external to you that will take over "your" life. It is YOU, yourself, the true Self of you, the *I* that you already are, even though you may not be consciously aware of it yet.

"God is your own being, and therefore *the infinite nature of God's being is the infinite nature of your own individual being.*"[28]

The celebrated sculptor Michelangelo once said, "I saw the angel in the marble and carved until I set him free." Similarly, as the sense of separation is carved away from us, Christhood, or divine sonship stands revealed.

BUT WHAT ABOUT THIS BODY?

Joel says, "The moment we realize: 'I am life eternal; I am pure Spirit, pure consciousness,' the question immediately arises, 'But what about this [physical] body?'"[29]

"You must come to the point where you understand your body and its function in your life; you must

---

27. *The Master Speaks:* Chapter 5, "The *I* That I Am."
28. *The Heart of Mysticism: Volume 2, The 1955 Infinite Way Letters:* Chapter 9: September, "The Deep Pool of Your Being."
29. *The Heart of Mysticism: Volume 4, The 1957 Infinite Way Letters:* Chapter 3: March, "Understanding the Body."

understand that *you* are not this *body*, and this *body* is not *you*: This body is an *instrument* through which you are functioning. You are the life of the body; you are the soul of the body; you are the intelligence of the body. You are that which uses the body as an instrument for your activities."[30]

In saying that you are not the body, Joel is not saying that you do not have a form. He is pointing out that in your true identity, you have *spiritual* form, which we might call the "Real body."

"Remember, the body itself is as spiritual as we are. This form which we see [the physical body] is a mental concept of that [Real] body ... We are never seeing the [Real] body; we are seeing a *human concept* of [the Real] body."[31]

"This does not mean that ... there is a real body and an unreal one. It means that the ... *only* body there is, is the real body, but what I am seeing is my *concept*."[32]

"What you physically see as your body represents your concept of body, but there is only one body, the body of God, and this is the secret of secrets."[33]

One of the most convincing ways that Joel helps us understand that we are not the physical body is by reminding us that even though our physical body changes, we maintain our identity.

---

30. ibid.
31. ibid.
32. *God the Substance of All Form:* Chapter 4, "Fulfillment of Consciousness."
33. *Conscious Union with God:* Chapter 6, "Teaching the Message."

"You are not body. You are life. You are consciousness. Though you keep paring your nails forever and forever, yet they continue to grow. Though every cell of your body drops off every year, year in and year out, yet you go right on—not dying, not passing on. You remain here and now. . . .

"You are not the [physical] body. You are that life, that mind, that soul—that's what constitutes you. God constitutes your being. Life-force constitutes your being. Soul constitutes your being, and therefore you are renewed and renewed and renewed. As often as your cells of the body may wear out, or the nails fall away or the hair falls away, you are eternally renewed without any death process."[34]

Think about the many forms your physical body has taken in this lifetime—infant form, toddler form, child form, adolescent form, adult form. Where are those body forms now? Despite the change in form, "I" am the same individual who had each of those forms. As an adult, I may be more knowledgeable, or more skilled, or more discerning than I was as a child or adolescent, but that is my rising state of consciousness. I am still the same individual "one," going by the same human name. If I were my body, wouldn't I have disappeared when one body form disappeared and another appeared?

BUT WHAT ABOUT THIS MIND?

While it is common to identify with the physical body, we may identify with the mind, too. We might believe that we are the mind that thinks, or even that we are the thoughts we have. But Joel makes it clear: "You are not your mind, any more than you

---

34. Recording 22A: 1953 New Hawaiian Series, "Major Principles of The Infinite Way."

are your body. You *possess* a mind, and you *possess* a body."[35] The mind is an instrument that we use.

"To understand the mind, first look at your body and realize that this body is your body, and that you can do with your body what you will. If you choose to walk to the right, your body has no power to resist you and walk downstairs. Your body has no power of its own. Your body cannot be moral or immoral; your hands cannot be honest or dishonest. Your body has no qualities of its own. It is merely a mechanical instrument fashioned for your use.

"Now go a step further and see that just as you have a body, so too, you have a mind. You can use your mind to develop a talent, a profession, or a business. It is your mind, and you can educate it in mathematics, music, art, science, or literature. You can keep your mind imbued with truth by filling it with scripture, spiritual and inspirational writings, or mystical poetry. You can keep your mind filled with truth or you can keep your mind filled with trash. You determine how many hours a day worthwhile literature is poured into your mind. You have the capacity to determine the nature of what goes into your mind. Just as your body is not a power unto itself, so your mind, also, is not a power. It cannot talk back to you; it has no control over you: you have control over it."[36]

"The mind is an instrument for something higher than itself. That Something is your Self, your true identity, and when It governs the mind and controls it,

35. Recording 340A: 1960 First London Closed Class, "I, No Power; No Darkness."
36. *The Journey Back to the Father's House*: Chapter 4, "The Temple."

you will find yourself at peace—perfect peace, a peace that passeth understanding."[37]

Joel called the mind an "avenue of awareness," meaning that it is through the mind that we can become aware of spiritual truth, aware of each other, aware of the laws, beauties, and rhythms of nature. We don't create these things; we become aware of them. Then we use the mind and body to bring forth that awareness into tangible forms—inventions, music, art, literature, architecture.

" The mind is an avenue of awareness; it is not a creative faculty. No one can create anything with the mind. Inventors, composers, artists, writers, poets never in their lives invented anything. They discovered them. Through the activity of the mind, they became aware of melodies, or they became aware of natural laws, or they became aware of influences, or they became aware of beauty in one form. They never created it; they became aware of it. The creative faculty is way down deep in the soul, and that Soul isn't a personal possession. It's God. It is God, the Soul of us, that really is the creative principle of existence. Through our mind we become aware of It."[38]

Mind produces its own image and likeness. In other words, if we fill our minds with truth, that truth externalizes as harmonious conditions. If we fill our minds with untruths, superstitions, rumors, deceits, fear, judgments, or anger and loathing, the mind produces conditions in our experience that reflect

37. *The Art of Spiritual Healing*: Chapter 4, "The Language of Spiritual Healing."
38. Recording 65B: 1954 Honolulu Lecture Series, "Meditation on One Power."

those things. Joel said that the mind is like a muffin tin. The muffins come out in the shape of the muffin tin.

"When you and I permit our minds to be filled with ignorance, superstition, and selfishness, that mind produces its own image and likeness, which is mirrored forth as the sins and diseases of the world; but when the mind is purified, so that it becomes an instrument for the pure Soul, then the mind produces the image and likeness of the Soul which is . . . spiritual perfection"[39]

Mind expresses as body, too:

"Because the mind will express whatever we put into it, by keeping it filled with God, it expresses as good in the body. Mind is the substance, or the essence, of which the body is formed, and it is for this reason that if we entertain truth in the mind, we experience harmony in the body. If we entertain evil, discord, and sin in the mind, we express these in the body. Whatever it is that we accept in mind, the body manifests. The mind itself is pure; the body itself is pure; but it is the kind of food we take into our minds that determines the nature of mind and body. . . . The more we feed the mind with the word of God, the more harmonious the body becomes."[40]

Many people allow the mind to control them. They say things like "I just can't stop worrying about it," or "I just can't get it out of my mind." It can be a great relief to know that the *I* that I truly

---

39. *The Thunder of Silence:* Chapter 5, "Transcending Mind."
40. *Living Now:* Chapter 6: "Mind Imbued with Truth."

am stands behind the mind and has control of it, even though it may take time to realize and demonstrate that.

We do not have to accept the theories, opinions, beliefs, and concepts that permeate human consciousness. We can renew our minds by learning the correct letter of truth, filling the mind with that truth, and contemplating it. Gradually, the correct letter of truth displaces erroneous beliefs and concepts and brings about a change in our state of consciousness. As Paul said, "Be not conformed to this world: but be ye transformed by the renewing of your mind."[41]

> " S piritual teaching involves an emptying out of the old 'bottles' to make way for the new wine. You cannot fill a vessel already full. You cannot receive a spiritual impartation in a mind filled with universal beliefs, theories, or opinions. Concepts and misconceptions must be cleared out of the mind so that it can become a transparency for truth."[42]

Joel emphasized that the mind we have *is* already the perfect Christ-mind, but that it has been contaminated and conditioned by the acceptance of erroneous beliefs and concepts. To "have that mind that was in Christ Jesus"[43] is not a matter of getting something that we don't have, but a matter of purifying the mind we have now.

> " T he mind which was in Christ Jesus is your mind and my mind in the degree in which it is illumined with a knowledge of truth. Every one of us has the mind which was in Christ Jesus, but not one of us has as yet

---

41. Romans 12:2.
42. *The Journey back to the Father's House:* Chapter 4, "The Temple."
43. Philippians 2:5.

attained a sufficient *depth of realization of it*. We think we have a mind of our own, and we come under the limitations which inevitably follow, believing that our capacity is limited by the circumstances of birth. Our mind, when illumined, *is* that mind which was in Christ Jesus, the same mind as the mind of every sage and seer throughout all time and from now unto eternity. Acknowledge that the mind which was in Christ Jesus is your mind and then, instead of doing your own thinking and planning, let the divine Wisdom become your mind, doing it for you, uttering Itself to you, expressing Itself within you, and speaking to you."[44]

THE HUMAN EXPERIENCE

We may be willing to accept the premise that in my true identity, I am pure Spirit, pure consciousness. We may be willing to consider what Joel says about the body and about the mind. But another question remains: What about this human experience?

Humanhood, or the human experience, is a state, or a stage, of unfolding consciousness; it is a phase on the path to enlightenment. Some have said, "We are spiritual beings having a human experience." But spiritual beings do not have human experiences, so it is more accurate to say that we are spiritual beings having a spiritual experience, but that we do not recognize or comprehend that spiritual experience as it truly is. We see it in a limited way, and we misinterpret it. The name we give to that misinterpretation is "human experience." Jesus called it "this world."

Joel put it this way:

---

44. *The Heart of Mysticism: Volume 5, The 1958 Infinite Way Letters*: Chapter 6: June, "Security Through God-Realization."

"Actually, that which we term the earth is heaven. Heaven, seen through three-dimensional eyes, is earth: the earth, seen through fourth dimensional eyes, is heaven. In other words, the very place whereon we stand is heaven."[45]

In our humanhood, we entertain a *sense* of a selfhood apart from God. We accept the beliefs of humanhood—that we have human parents; that we were born; that we will die. We believe that we are limited in intelligence and limited in resources, and that we must struggle to survive. We look outside ourselves for our good and for our fulfillment. We identify with a physical body and believe that it controls our life. We allow our mind to manipulate us. We experience fear. All of this is the result of ignorance of our true identity—the true nature of individual being.

Humanhood does not become spiritual. Even attaining so-called good humanhood does not return us to the consciousness of our true spiritual being and enable us to experience the universe of Spirit in which we actually live. Humanhood must be "put off" and left behind. In other words, we can *evolve* out of humanhood as the light of truth takes root in our consciousness. In the human state of consciousness, even though we might be living in ignorance of our true identity, that ignorance does not change the absolute truth of our being one with God any more than the true identity of a prince would change if he were kidnapped and brought up as a pauper. Oneness with God is our true, original, eternal state of being. The goal of a spiritual path is to help us evolve out of that human state of consciousness and awaken to our true spiritual identity in Christhood.

---

45. *Living the Illumined Life*: Chapter 3, "The Sword of the Spirit."

CHAPTER 6

THE NATURE OF ERROR

IN THE INFINITE WAY, the term "error" generally refers to anything that appears to be evil, negative, or discordant, such as disease, death, lack, limitation, extreme weather events, wars, oppressive governments, and so on. The dictionary defines error as "an unintentional deviation from truth or accuracy; a mistake, a misconception, or a delusion." So the term "error" is quite appropriate, because Joel teaches that error is a mistake or delusion, or in other words, "an unintentional deviation from truth," due to the human ignorance of spiritual truth. Just as we can say that cold is the *absence* of heat, and darkness is the *absence* of light, we might say that error is the *absence* of truth.

Since error, or evil, is one of the most perplexing things in human experience, every spiritual teaching should address the nature of error. People have always asked, "Why do bad things happen?" and "How can we stop them?" Rarely is there a satisfactory answer. Joel confronts the issue head on, and although at first, some may not fully grasp or even understand his answer, he does have an answer, and it differs radically from other teachings.

" I don't know of a single religion in all of the world that does not acknowledge that God is the only power. Every religion does that, and because of that, they have to acknowledge that God 'calls home' His beloved ones, sometimes when they are only two, five, ten, or fifteen years of age. . . . You've heard ministers tell you at funerals, 'This is the will of God. God is calling His loved ones home.' You have seen people in terrible afflictions and heard that this is the will of God: 'The will of God is inscrutable. We can't see why this is, but God knows it's for our good.'

"[You have heard that] God is the cause of violent acts—storms at sea, hurricanes, volcanoes. That's why insurance companies don't have to pay off on them— they're 'acts of God.' Now how does the church say that God is the only power in the face of all of these things? By acknowledging that God is responsible for them! In that sense then, if you judge by appearances, you must acknowledge that there are sick people, sinful people, dying people. You must acknowledge that there are accidents; that there are all kinds of natural disasters and manmade disasters; and behind all of this you must acknowledge God, if God is the only power. Now there is no other way out of that dilemma, and that is the way the church has taken: God is the only power and therefore, God is calling his dearly beloved home. . . .

"The Master, Christ Jesus, declares that his mission on earth, the spiritual mission, is to heal the sick and raise the dead, to open the eyes of the blind, to open the ears of the deaf. And yet, we are told that blindness, and deafness, and sickness, and death, is the will of God. But did Jesus come to destroy the will of God, to overcome the will of God? Nonsense, isn't it? But it is a dilemma from which there is no escape if you judge by appearances.

"Now, there have been spiritually illumined people on earth who have seen that there is no death, and some who have even seen that there is no birth; some who have seen that there is no disease on earth, no reality to any of these negative appearances. . . . Gautama, the Buddha, founded his entire revelation not on what God is, but on what error isn't. The revelation that came to him under that Bodhi Tree was that all of these appearances are illusion; are not reality; are not taking place in time or space. They are taking place only in mortal concept—a universal mortal concept, but a mortal concept. Jesus saw that vision [too] because he looked right at Pilate and said, 'Thou couldst have no power,'[1] although all appearances testify to the fact that he [Pilate] was the ruler of the land and had all power.

"Jesus was able to look at disease and say, 'What did hinder you? Rise, pick up your bed and walk.'[2] He was able to look at sin and say, 'Neither do I condemn thee.'[3] I don't think that Jesus condoned sin. He recognized that sin, as sin, doesn't exist. Very little of that principle came to light in the following years, . . . and so, we have very little on the subject [of error] until the original *Science and Health*.[4]

"The original *Science and Health* made clear again, for the first time in centuries . . . that God is the only power, and that these *appearances* of discord do not have reality. . . . There is but one power and that is God, but God is *not* the author of death. God is *not* the creator of death. God is *not* the creator of accidents. God is *not* the creator of storms at sea. God is *not* the creator of volcanoes and tornadoes. That is absolutely fantastic! You would have to go back to your Hebrew God to believe any such thing. You would have to give up your Christianity which says 'God is love' to believe that there's

---

1. John 19:11.
2. John 5:8.
3. John 8:11.
4. *Science* and *Health* is by Mary Baker Eddy, Founder of Christian Science.

anything loving about a ship going down in the middle of the ocean, or an airplane falling out of the sky, for any reason whatsoever, even for an inscrutable reason."[5]

As you can see, Joel was quite willing to take on the issue of error, or evil. The nature of error was revealed to him; he had the realization of it; and he demonstrated the principle countless times in his extensive healing ministry.

"Now, it has been left to The Infinite Way to reveal to the world the source of all evil. You could ask ministers, rabbis, priests, of any denomination the source of evil, and you would get the answer that this is not known. And up until this message of The Infinite Way, it has not been known how evil originated, and how it is perpetuated, and how it may be overcome. And in the days to come, it will be this revelation which you will prove, first in your individual experience, and then in a wider circle until you will see how it embraces the world.

"You will learn that every bit of evil that has ever touched you in your life has come from a universal belief with which you had nothing to do; a universal belief that there are two powers—good and evil."[6]

REALITY AND UNREALITY

Those who are new to The Infinite Way may be shocked to hear Joel say, "these appearances of discord do not have reality," so it is important to understand what Joel means by "real."

---

5. Recording 142A: 1956 First Steinway Hall Practitioner Class, "Above and Beyond Thought or Thing."
6. Recording 343B: 1960 Holland Closed Class, "The Vision of The Infinite Way."

"In our work, the word 'real' or 'reality' pertains only to that which is spiritual, eternal, immortal, infinite. Only that which is of God is called real, or reality. And now be sure of this: you cannot see, hear, taste, touch, or smell reality. . . . Reality pertains only to that which is spiritual, is of Spirit, Soul, God, and therefore must be spiritually discerned, spiritually understood. It requires the faculty of Soul to behold reality.

"The unreal, or unreality, is anything, whether to our sense harmonious or inharmonious, that is not permanent, that is not God-governed, God-maintained and God-sustained. . . . If you can see, hear, taste, touch and smell it, it is not a part of reality, regardless of how good or harmonious or fine it may be. Reality pertains only to that which is discerned through the inner awareness. . . .

"When we speak of sin or disease as unreal, or unrealities, we do not mean nonexistent. We do not mean that we are just fooling ourselves or using our imagination in saying it is unreal or untrue. It is not a denial of the so-called existence of these things. It is a denial of their existence **as a part of God or reality**. . . . Now then, with that distinction in mind, you can accept this premise of metaphysical and spiritual healing ministries: that all sin, disease, lack, limitation are unreal. They are no part of reality."[7]

"The word "reality" . . . means that which is permanent, that which is eternal, that which is infinite, that which always has been and always will be. In that sense of the word, you would understand instantly the unreal nature of disease. There was a time when the disease did not exist and there will be a time when it will

---

7. Recording 17A: 1952 Honolulu Closed Class, "Spiritual Healing."

not exist. It is not real, because it has no substance to maintain or sustain it. It exists only as a finite sense, as a false sense, in the same way in which two times two are five exists not as reality, not as an entity or identity; but as an appearance, belief, or illusion, or a false sense of mathematics."[8]

THE NATURE OF ERROR IS DERIVED FROM THE NATURE OF GOD

Just as the nature of God as omnipresence gives us the nature of individual being, the nature of God as omnipotence gives us the nature of error. If God is infinite, and if God is all-power, there can be no other power.

" Good is omnipotence, and omnipotence means all-power, and all-power means there is no other power. It doesn't mean a great power *overcoming* other powers. Omnipotence means an all-power, besides which there is no [other] power."[9]

Many people affirm their belief in an omnipotent God but fail to follow that to its logical conclusion. For example, even though they say that God is omnipotent, they also believe that disease has power.

" How many hymns have been sung and how many words have been written about omnipotence! But there is scarcely a soul who sings about omnipotence or talks about it who believes it, because to almost everyone,

---

8. *The Master Speaks:* Chapter 13, "Individual Consciousness."
9. Recording 497A: 1962 Stockholm Closed Class, "Sowing to the Spirit—Or to the Flesh."

omnipotence means a mighty power *over* other powers. But that is not omnipotence. 'Omni' means 'all.'"[10]

In other words, if God is infinite, there is only God, and so there is no need for power in the sense of power *over* anything. When Joel speaks of God as a power, he is referring to God as the creative, maintaining, and sustaining power, not as a great power that battles or overcomes other powers.

" You'd be surprised how we sing hymns to the almighty God and then fear a flu germ. We sing to the all-powerful, all-mighty, supreme God and fear a pimple. You see, Omnipotence means the all, the *only* power, and Omnipresence means that It is here and now where I am."[11]

Furthermore, if God is the one and *only* power, there can be nothing else that has power.

" If God is omnipotence, then what power is there in any physical, mental, moral, or financial condition? If God is all-power, can there be a power in any negative condition? Every time we become aware of some negative, material, or mental power, we must realize the truth of Omnipotence: *Spirit is the only power; spiritual law is the only power; spiritual grace is the only power.*"[12]

Then how are we to regard all the evils that we see in human experience? We have a choice. We can take Joel's revelation and accept that since God is the infinite all-power, evil appearances

---

10. *A Message for the Ages:* Chapter 2, "God and Prayer."
11. Recording 356B: 1960 England Open Class, "Putting Up the Sword Is the Secret."
12. *A Parenthesis in Eternity:* Chapter 11, "The Nature of Spiritual Power."

and discords cannot have power, despite their *seeming* power. We can work with that and see if we can prove it in our own experience. The other choice is to give up the premise that God is infinite and the *only* power and presence and say that God is *not* omnipotent; that there is something other than God that has power. In other words, we can adopt the belief that there is God *and* there is something other than God. Said another way, we can adopt the belief in two powers, good and evil.

Joel acknowledges that evil *seems* to be a tremendous power in human experience but teaches us not to judge by appearances. To emphasize that error has no power, he uses synonyms for error, or evil, that mean "unreal," such as "hypnotism," "mesmerism," "universal belief," "illusion," "appearance," "claim," "mirage," "nothingness," and "mental suggestion." Joel says that when we believe that error, or evil, has power, we are "hypnotized" or "mesmerized."

" To illustrate this nothingness of evil, we may well ponder the Oriental story as given in *The Infinite Way* of the man who mistook the rope for a snake:

'About 500 B.C. it was written: "It easily happens that a man, when taking a bath, steps upon a wet rope and imagines that it is a snake. Horror will overcome him, and he will shake from fear, anticipating in his thought all the agonies caused by the serpent's venomous bite. What a relief does this man experience when he sees that the rope is no snake. The cause of his fright lies in his error, his ignorance, his illusion. If the true nature of the rope is recognized, his tranquility of mind will come back to him; he will feel relieved; he will be joyful and happy. This is the state of mind of one who has recognized that there is no personal self; that the cause of all his troubles, cares and vanities is a mirage, a shadow, a dream.'"

"To material sense, sin and disease appear as real entities having substance, law, cause and effect. To material sense, both sin and disease seem personal and tenacious. But to spiritual consciousness, both sin and disease are unrealities in the sense that they exist only as the product of a universal belief of a selfhood apart from God."[13]

"Give it [evil] any name you like. You can call it devil or mortal mind, or you can call it appearance, or you can call it claim, or you can call it illusion. Call it anything you want, as long as when you call it, you are at the same time saying 'nothingness.'"[14]

No illusion is, or ever can be, externalized. For example, railroad tracks appear to come together in the distance. But this appearance is an illusion that exists in the mind; it does not exist as an external reality. The tracks do not come together. The perception that the tracks come together does not make them come together. It is an erroneous perception.

At this point, you may feel a rightness about what Joel taught about the nature of error, even though you may not fully grasp it. Or you may just be outright baffled because what you are reading is so different from your experience and belief. In either case, just consider Joel's revelation about error. The nature of error is not an easy principle to understand or to accept. Even so, Joel's revelation is a fascinating alternative that does give an answer

13. *Spiritual Interpretation of Scripture*: "Ruth and Naomi."
14. Recording 374B: 1960 Adelaide Closed Class, "One."

to the perennial questions about evil. It explains why traditional prayer often is not effective—the prayers seek to change a condition that has reality only in thought. Joel said that such prayer is like trying to overcome the mirage on the desert or trying to overcome two times two is five. We cannot change something that does not exist.

"When we recognize that evil, regardless of whether it appears as sin, disease, lack, wars, or death, is but one evil, mesmeric suggestion or hypnotism, we have found our freedom from these discords. In other words, the specific errors we behold or experience are not realities which must be fought or destroyed; they are not powers requiring some deific prayer or personage to act; they are mirage or nothingness and need only to be acknowledged as such to reveal their impotence. . . .

"Let us take as an illustration the vaudeville hypnotist who, as part of his act, invites members of the audience to come up on the stage to be hypnotized. Then he suggests to them that there is a white poodle on the stage, which he wishes the mesmerized person to chase off into the wings. Sometimes the white poodle goes off stage with little effort, but at other times it proves to be very obstreperous and difficult to make obey. Let us suppose now that our hypnotized friend recognizes a metaphysician in the audience and requests help in removing his white poodle. Remember, to the hypnotized man the white poodle exists as a real entity, an actual presence, and he wants it removed. To the metaphysician, however, who is not hypnotized and sees clearly, there is no poodle there to be removed: only a mesmeric suggestion to be recognized as such, and this recognition brings the awakening and the disappearance of the white poodle. . . .

"In the same sense, every problem, whether of health, supply, sin or fear, is real to the deluded sufferer, but to the metaphysician, these exist only as the non-existent 'white poodle,' and he heals all manner of error through this understanding of the unreal nature of what appears as evil conditions of mind, body or purse."[15]

ONLY IN THE PRESENCE OF ILLUMINED CONSCIOUSNESS IS ERROR NOT A POWER

Sometimes people who are on a metaphysical path say, "Evil is not a power." Seeing an accident, they may declare, "Oh, we know this has no power." Joel emphasized that this is only a half-truth. Once we understand that error is not a power, we must quickly add that error is not a power *ONLY in the presence of illumined consciousness.* In the human state of consciousness, error certainly *seems* to have power.

" The full truth is that *in the presence of the Christ, in the presence of illumined consciousness,* there is no power in any form of error, evil, or discord. If the truth that error is not power were all that is necessary, it would just disappear, wherever it might seem to be, but it disappears only when it touches illumined consciousness, the consciousness of that individual who has received spiritual Grace, realization, illumination."[16]

" It is the height of foolishness to go around making affirmations that food has no power, that climate, in-

---

15. *Spiritual Interpretation of Scripture:* "From Law to Grace."
16. *Seek Ye First:* Chapter 7, "The Practicality of Illumination."

fection, contagion, and depression have no power. It is utter nonsense. They do, and as long as there is a human picture, they will have power. But they have no power, they have no presence, and they do not even exist *where the spirit of the Lord is realized.*"[17]

"**I**n *the presence of God,* evil is not power. *In the presence of God,* error cannot exist, whether it is a condition of weather, a condition of food, a condition of poison, a condition of bullets or bombs. None of these have power *in the presence of God.* You see, all error has power. If you don't think so, just think of the way the world is in fear of atomic bombs today, and you will know how much power bombs have, and fear has. Or, let the newspapers talk about a flu epidemic on the way and see how much power the flu epidemic has and the fear of it has, and you will know that error has power. But, *in the presence of the Christ,* error has no power. And it makes no difference now whether it's germs, bombs, fear, or anything else. In the presence of the Almighty, there are no other powers. There cannot be an Almighty and other powers too."[18]

ERROR IS IMPERSONAL

One of the most surprising aspects of the nature of error as it was revealed to Joel is that error, or evil, is impersonal. This means that evil is not *in* or *of* a person and does not arise *from* a person, and that we cannot blame ourselves or others for it.

---

17. *The Only Freedom:* Chapter 7, "Where the Spirit of the Lord Is, There Is Liberty."
18. Recording 552A: 1964 Portland Special Class, "Between Two Worlds."

"Remember that all evil is impersonal; it is not *in* you or *of* you or *through* you. You may be at this moment manifesting it by acceptance, but it does not have its origin in you, and therefore, it is no part of you. It is like putting some dirt in this clean glass of water and then saying, 'It's dirty water.' It isn't dirty water; it never becomes dirty water. The moment you take the dirt out, you'll see the water is as clean as ever. It was always dirt in the water, not dirty water. The dirt and the water are always separable and divisible."[19]

"One of the most important of the principles revealed to me was the impersonal cause and nature of evil. All evil, regardless of its name or nature, is impersonal. That means that it is not *your* wrong thinking that has caused your trouble—not *your* envy, jealousy, or malice, not *your* sensuality, *your* lack of gratitude, not *your* anything. Not a single thing in you is responsible for any of your ills. . . . The evil or error that is finding expression in you, whether as disease, an evil trait of character, or as a false appetite, has absolutely nothing to do with you. It did not begin in you, and you will never root it out of you. You never will."[20]

Then where does evil come from? Joel explains that evil has its rise in an *impersonal* source, a belief, a universal sense of evil.

"Evil has its origin in something that for the moment we may call the carnal mind. If the term 'carnal mind' means nothing to you, call it Satan. If these terms do not appeal to you, call it an appearance, a claim, or

---

19. Recording 335B: 1960 Toronto Private Closed Class, "Advancing on the Path."
20. *Man Was Not Born to Cry*: Chapter 3, "The Truth That Makes Free."

an illusion. The name you give it is unimportant. The important thing is to know that evil of whatever name or nature, stems from a *universal impersonal* source."[21]

He explains further that, although we give it a label, this impersonal source is *not* a reality or an entity, meaning that it is not of God, infinite good, and therefore has nothing to sustain it:

"Call it carnal mind or mortal mind if you like, or devil or Satan; give it any name you like, as long as you understand it to be an *impersonal* source. And then take the next step and realize since God did not create that source, it has no law; it has no life; it has no cause, no substance, no activity, no avenue, no channel of expression. In other words, it is a nothingness."[22]

Sometimes people find it difficult to accept the teaching that evil is not personal because it contradicts the universal belief that individuals are responsible for evil actions. For example, people believe that evil is *in* the terrorist; that evil was *in* Hitler. Joel is not saying that in the human realm, we should not hold people to account. He is saying that from the spiritual view, wrongdoing is the result of spiritual ignorance, and that the evil does not have its rise *in* any individual. We are born into a human consciousness that already has accepted the belief that there is God *and* some evil power.

"Has not history proved that the assassination of kings and queens and emperors has never stopped tyranny? It never does and it never can because the evil is not personal. As rapidly as one person is eliminated,

---

21. *Man Was Not Born to Cry*: Chapter 3, "The Truth That Makes Free."
22. Recording 261B: 1959 Hawaiian Village Open Class, "The Nature of Error."

we come face to face with the same evil in the next person. But the realization that evil is always impersonal could do much to free the world from all the dictators of the world."[23]

"A person is not evil even if he appears as the most ruthless and tyrannical dictator the world has ever known. He will be evil to us if we see him as evil, but he cannot be that to us if we see him as he is in his true identity and realize that the evil we are beholding is not an evil person: it is a mesmeric influence which is being accepted as reality."[24]

"Whatever evil may be expressing itself through you or me at any given moment is the degree in which we are accepting carnal mind as power and either ignorantly or carelessly permitting it to function in us."[25]

Joel had an extraordinarily successful prison ministry, and he said that his success came from his ability to impersonalize evil and to see the prisoners not as criminals, but as people who, through ignorance, had found themselves in the grip of the impersonal source of evil. He did not bring an attitude of condemnation or judgment to his work; his ministry was to enlighten the prisoners about their true identity.

---

23. *The Heart of Mysticism: Volume 6, The 1959 Infinite Way Letters:* Chapter 10: October, "Freeing Ourselves from Universal Claims."
24. *Realization of Oneness:* Chapter 3, "Get Thee Hence, Satan."
25. *Spiritual Power of Truth:* Chapter 5, "Universal Hypnotism."

HOW ARE WE TO HANDLE THE APPEARANCE OF ERROR?

Joel says that as long as we are in the human state of consciousness, we will always see two powers—good and evil—and he explains what we can do:

" There is only one power. There is no power of evil. There is no power of sin. There is no power of disease. There is no power of lack or limitation. There is only one power. . . . In other words, you have to accept—even if you do it only with the mind—that God is the only power. God made all that was made. Anything that God did not make was not made. And so, we have God as the one power; God as the only power.

"Now, because we are intelligent people, we have the right to say, 'Yes, with my mind I have accepted that, but also with my mind I must say this—that I don't see evidence of it.' There is a great power of disease in the world. There is a great power of wars and atomic bombs in the world. There is a great power of sin. Very often there is even a great power of depression and lack and unemployment in the world.

"This world *seems* to be made up of powers of infection, powers of contagion, powers of hereditary diseases, powers of evil in many ways, and that is true. As long as we are dealing with the human world in a human way, there will be two powers: the power of good and the power of evil, and the power of evil will be the dominant power. "[26]

---

26. Recording 65B: 1954 Honolulu Lecture Series, "Meditation on One Power."

What do we do about it? How do we rise into the consciousness of one power? Joel continues:

" **N** ow, to transcend this, to come into a state of existence where . . . you find only one power—that is something that is brought about by you individually in your experience. You can be taught how to do it, but no one can do it for you. That becomes an activity of your own consciousness . . . You must learn to do it. Now, here is one of the ways. Start with the theme that God is one. God is one. 'Hear, O Israel: The Lord our God is one.'[27] God is one. Thou shalt have no other gods; no other powers; no other laws but one.

"As you go about your life during the day, you are greeted either in the newspaper or on the radio with some news of a distressing nature about international affairs, and here is where you begin the practice of truth. It becomes necessary as you read or hear this news, to remind yourself that since God is one, and God is the only power, the only power operating in this universe is the power of good.

"Now, we know about these other appearances. We know about the claim that dictators have powers, or bad senators or congressmen have power, or a bad this or that has power. We know all about that. Ours is a *holding to a spiritual truth*, not the appearance as it is in the news. The spiritual truth is: God alone is power. Now, you bring this into your experience by not acknowledging anything but God in all your ways. So in that instance, you will acknowledge, 'God is the only power operating in this universe.'

---

27. Deuteronomy 6:4.

"The next thing, your attention is brought to some form of sickness, whether of your own or another's. It makes no difference. The responsibility rests with you, the moment you become conscious of illness, to bring to light the realization, 'God, Spirit, is the only power and the only law. God is the only law. There cannot then be a law of disease.' . . .

"When you adopt for yourself God as one, you will have only *one* law; and that law will be the law of God, and it will be the law of good, and it will be omniactive and omnipresent in your experience. But no one can do this for you. This you must do for yourself."[28]

Joel goes on to say that we must make this mental adjustment with every appearance of evil, regardless of whether we believe it affects us personally or not.

"Again, in your day you will be faced with the temptation of death. It makes no difference whether you are being told about the death of a friend or relative or someone in a volcano country or plague country or a country devoid of food. Always, there isn't a day goes by that the presence of death isn't consciously brought to your awareness. Now, just because it isn't you who are in danger of dying today, do not neglect this opportunity. Do not put it aside as if, 'Well, that doesn't interest me at the present moment.' Indeed, it does interest you. It interests you at any moment that it is presented to you, because either you will let it come into your consciousness, or you will rule it out, and if you rule it out now, you may never have to meet it again.

---

28. Recording 65B: 1954 Honolulu Lecture Series, "Meditation on One Power."

"Now, at the merest suggestion of the danger of death or the presence of death, bring your theme to bear: God is one. One what? Well, you know God is life. Oh, God is life! Then life is eternal; life is immortal; life is infinite; never beginning and never ending, since life is God. God is life, and there is only one God. Therefore, there is only one life."[29]

Eventually, this practice becomes automatic because every time you do it, you are building your consciousness of one power. As Joel says:

"As you persist in this throughout the day, the night, the week, the month, gradually you get to a point as you would if you took up driving an automobile today, and you had to watch your left foot and your right foot and your left hand and your right hand. For a week you might have to watch those, but at the end of a month you would be driving a car without ever thinking of your hands or feet.

"And so it is with this, that at the end of a month, you would find that you didn't have to again consciously think about God as one or God as life. You wouldn't have to think of that at all, because it would be so much a part of your consciousness that the moment the opposite touched you, it would be almost as if you saw a line going down that way, erasing it without any conscious effort on your part . . .

"Do you see why I say that no one can do this for you? This is a practice that takes place within you until such time as the word 'one' becomes so embedded in you that you would never accept these appearances as they

29. ibid.

come to your consciousness. . . . God is truth and truth omnipresent in your consciousness is the law of elimination to every form of discord in your experience."[30]

With his revelation on the nature of error, Joel is inviting us to look at error, or evil, from an entirely different perspective. He asks us to consider his revelation with an open mind, to work with it and see if we get a feeling of "rightness" about it, even if at first we do not fully comprehend it.

For a more in-depth look at the nature of error, Chapter 11, "A Plan for Study," recommends several excellent recordings.

---

30. ibid.

CHAPTER 7

THE NATURE OF PRAYER

FOR MANY PEOPLE, prayer means speaking to God, petitioning for help or favors, or trying to influence God to do something. Often, bargaining is involved. When Joel teaches about the nature of prayer, one of the aspects he addresses is how prayer in The Infinite Way differs from the commonly accepted meaning of prayer.

Just as Joel invited us to look at our beliefs about God and our beliefs about ourselves, he asks us to examine our beliefs about prayer.

"When we speak of prayer on the spiritual path, we are not speaking of prayer as we have been taught. We have not been given an understanding of prayer until we have changed our entire concept on the subject of prayer. To illustrate this, the prayer of petition, in which we ask God for food or clothing or housing; in which we ask God to sell our real estate or be sure that our stocks don't go down; the prayer in which we ask God to heal our friends and relatives—this has no place in the life of the spiritual student. The prayer of petition is as outmoded as yesterday's newspaper. . . .

"For those seeking spiritual illumination, for those seeking contact with their Source, such prayer must quickly be discarded, and therein lies the first difficulty: habit. We have been so in the habit of praying to God, if not actually preying upon God!"[1]

"We cannot add the truth about prayer to our former concepts of prayer. If our prayers have not been answered, let us *have the humility to begin to discard* all that we have ever known and take the attitude, 'I do not know how to pray.' . . . No progress will be made until we have completely emptied out all ideas of what we believe prayer to be."[2]

OMNISCIENCE GIVES US THE NATURE OF PRAYER

Joel points out that in The Infinite Way, prayer comes from the nature of God as omniscience, and this accounts for a major difference between the customary meaning of prayer and the meaning of prayer in The Infinite Way.

"The word Omniscience reminds us of what we have been doing in our prayers. Have we not been guilty of telling God something? Have we not been reminding God of something? Have we not been asking something of God that we think God does not know anything about? Have we not been telling God of someone who needs Him?

"Think what you do when you go to God with anything that you wish to convey to this Omniscience, to this All-wisdom, All-knowledge, All-power, All-presence; and then you will quickly learn how to transform your

---

1. Recording 468B: 1962 Chicago Closed Class, "Preparation for Prayer."
2. *The Altitude of Prayer*: Chapter 2: "Creating A Vacuum for the Inflow of the Spirit."

prayer into a righteous prayer, a prayer that is a resting back in God in an inner assurance that 'before they call, I will answer; and while they are yet speaking, I will hear;'[3] that before you know your need, He knows it, and it is His 'good pleasure to give you the kingdom.'[4] Think of how this will change your prayer as you learn to look upon God as the great All-wisdom, All-presence, and All-power."[5]

"You have to become used to the idea that God is infinite intelligence, and that God is divine love, and if God is infinite intelligence, He needs no advice from you or me. He needs no entreaties from you or me. He needs no instructions from you or me, for He is the infinite, all-knowing mind, the wisdom, the great enough wisdom, to form this universe, to maintain it, to sustain it, to give us the spiritual laws by which we live."[6]

Many still think of God as something separate and apart from themselves; as some far-off entity who supposedly "knows our need before we do." Joel dispels this notion with this simple statement:

"Omniscience knows all, and It knows all about every individual because omniscience *is* the allness of every individual."[7]

---

3. Isaiah 65:24.
4. Luke 12:32.
5. *The Contemplative Life*: Chapter 6, "Contemplative Meditation."
6. Recording 372A: 1960 Perth Closed Class, "Going on to Prayer and Meditation."
7. *Beyond Words and Thoughts*: Chapter 8, "The Way of Grace."

He elaborates:

"No one would ever pray to God if they knew God or knew the nature of God, and I mean pray in the way in which orthodox people have been taught to pray. . . . What makes it so difficult is that regardless of what our religious background has been or has not been, we still think of God consciously or subconsciously or unconsciously as if there were a God separate and apart from our own being. It is only when you realize, 'God is my own consciousness' that all of a sudden the shoulders relax and you breathe a deep sigh and say, 'Oh! There is no reason to take thought anymore. My consciousness knows all about me and all about my needs.'"[8]

PRAYER IS NEVER AN ATTEMPT TO INFLUENCE GOD

Conventional prayer relies on a belief that our prayers can influence God. But Joel emphasized that prayer is never trying to influence God in any way, never telling God what we need, never begging or pleading with God.

"If God is omnipotent and omniscient, all-power and all-wisdom, what chance would anyone have to influence God to do something that God is not at this second doing? Do you think that by taking thought you could make God do something that God is not now doing? Do you think you could move God out of Its orbit and hold back the sunlight for five minutes for some reason or other, or have the sun set five minutes sooner or later?"[9]

---

8. *Consciousness Transformed*: March 31, 1963, "*My* Consciousness."
9. *Spiritual Discernment*: Chapter 11, "The Infinite Way of Life."

"As this is being written, there is no sun in the heavens—it is nighttime, yet there is no trace of fear about tomorrow. It would be useless to pray that the sun rise tomorrow, simply because God requires no information or prayer from us. God will go about Its business of governing this universe, and in due time the sun will rise. Praying in the manner of petitioning and beseeching will not change the orderly rhythm of God's universe. God's work is done; God's laws are in operation; God's processes are already at work. That which *is*, divinely and eternally *is*, and we cannot influence God to make it so, or to prevent its being so.

"This gives us quite a different concept of God than many we have entertained heretofore. We have felt that it was important and necessary that we acquaint God with our needs and the needs of the world. The Master has told us, '. . . your Father knoweth what things ye have need of, before ye ask him,'[10] and '. . . it is your Father's good pleasure to give you the kingdom.'[11] This should have taught us that the nature of prayer is a realization of the nature of God, of God's laws and God's love, and that the prayer which attempts to tell or ask God is not of much avail."[12]

"Once you recognize God as infinite Intelligence and divine Love, the whole nature of your prayer will change. This, you, yourself, will realize as you learn to approach God, not in the nature of a power that you would beseech for favors or ask for gifts, but rather in the knowledge that you can rest in that same realization in which

---

10. Matthew 6:8.
11. Luke 12:32.
12. *The Heart of Mysticism: Volume 2, The 1955 Infinite Way Letters*: Chapter 7: July, "Meditation for Beginners."

David rested when he was enabled to say, 'The Lord is my shepherd, I shall not want.'[13] . . . No need there to beseech God, to ask or to beg of God, but rather to abide in the awareness that *He leadeth* me beside the still waters, *He maketh* me to lie down in green pastures."[14]

Joel is not suggesting that we simply do nothing and take the attitude "Oh, let God take care of it," unless of course, we have the realized experience of God's presence. He is saying that we must consciously and constantly entertain this truth of Omniscience, infinite intelligence, in our awareness, and that prayer should be in accord with that truth.

WHAT CAN WE PRAY FOR?

Many who embrace conventional prayer believe that they can pray for material things. On the contrary, Joel teaches that we never pray to God for material things, and he often says, "Pray for anything you like, as long as it is not of this world."[15] Praying for material things is "praying amiss," and such prayer is unanswered.

" As long as we understand that God is spirit, we must go to God only for spiritual things. . . . Jesus taught that the Father loves those who worship him in spirit and in truth, not in temples, not in holy mountains, but in spirit and in truth. That is virtually the same thing as saying that in worshiping or praying to God, we should not pray for material things because God is spirit. What we should do is pray in spirit and in truth, pray for the

---

13. Psalm 23:1.
14. *The Heart of Mysticism: Volume 4, The 1957 Infinite Way Letters:* Chapter 2: February, "Major Principles of The Infinite Way."
15. Recording 114B: 1955 Kailua Study Group, "How to Pray."

revelation of truth, pray for the revelation and unfold-ment of spirit, pray for a realization of the presence of God. Then what? All these things will be added unto us: food, raiment, housing. All these things will be added unto us if we pray for spiritual things."[16]

In other words, we pray only for spiritual blessings, but when we receive those spiritual blessings, we will perceive them, or said another way, they will appear to us, as forms that we can understand—tangible material forms, circumstances, or conditions that meet our needs.

"The key to effectual prayer is to pray for anything we want that does not have a physical body or form, that is, corporeality. We have a right to pray for anything in the spiritual realm: spiritual light, spiritual wisdom, spiritual truth, spiritual bread, spiritual wine, spiritual water, spiritual resurrection, anything in the nature of incorporeal substance, being, or form. As we do that, our prayers will be answered and will appear [to us] in the tangible form of food, clothing, housing, and compan-ionship, and all the things that have corporeal form."[17]

TRUE PRAYER IS RECEPTIVE LISTENING

In conventional prayer, the person who is praying often has the mindset that they are speaking to God. From time to time, Joel himself speaks about his "conversations" with God, and so he is not in any way disparaging the feeling or the sense of talking to God. However, when Joel teaches about true prayer, the high form of prayer, he is clear that prayer is not speaking to God but

---

16. *God Formed Us for His Glory:* Chapter 9, "The Inner Meaning of Living the Spiritual Life."
17. *The Art of Spiritual Living:* Chapter 4, "The Hidden Kingdom."

going to God only for the joy of communion, and then listening—listening for "the still small voice."[18] In other words, true prayer is listening, not speaking.

" Prayer is not the words we speak, but the still, small Voice of God uttering Itself to us.... The highest sense of prayer is *listening*, not speaking or thinking, but listening." [19]

" Let us endeavor to outgrow the belief that prayer is acquainting God with our troubles, or that prayer is asking for blessings of some specific nature. Let us, rather, think of prayer as an attitude of holy communion, in which we rise into the higher atmosphere of Spirit, wherein prayer is recognized to be the Word of God which is to unfold from within. How vastly different is our attitude when all problems are left outside the door, and we turn to God solely for the privilege of sitting at the foot of the Throne, thereby letting the glories of God's grace be unfolded and revealed!"[20]

" Prayer, then, is an impartation which I receive from God. It is not a message that I send out to God or up to God or within to God. In other words, prayer is not a message from me to God. Prayer is a message received by me *from* God, and since the kingdom of God is within me, the prayer, the word of God, must likewise be received *within* me. Therefore, my attitude of prayer always must be, 'Speak, Lord, thy servant heareth,'[21] and

18. 1 Kings 19:12.
19. *Living by Grace:* Chapter 3: "The Christ Ministry."
20. *The Heart of Mysticism: Volume 3, The 1956 Infinite Way Letters:* Chapter 3: March, "The Part We Play."
21. 1 Samuel 3:10.

then I must adopt that listening ear. 'Speak, Lord, thy servant heareth,' and prayer then becomes an attitude as well as an altitude. . . .

"It becomes necessary to rise so high in consciousness that the still, small voice can be heard. You cannot hear the still, small voice when you are way down on a low level of life—the level of self, the level of selfishness, the level of personal interest. Life must be lived on a higher altitude."[22]

While Joel used terms like "Speak, Lord," or the "still, small voice," or "the Word of God," he explained that an impartation received in prayer might not come audibly in words. It might come as a state of awareness, a feeling of the Presence, an inner release of some kind, or even just a deep breath. Some people experience light or fragrance. The "voice of God" can "speak" in any form, and it comes to each one in an individual way.

"It is possible to see visions or to hear the still small voice; and then there are times when the presence makes itself known through the activity of smell, and even of touch. We may feel a touch on the shoulder, the head, or on the cheek. At other times, the fragrance of flowers may be noticed. There is no way to limit God and feel that he can appear in one way only. God can appear in any form, and probably we can understand that best by recalling that when Joan of Arc was asked, 'Does God speak to you in French?' Her reply was, 'I do not know in what language God speaks, but I hear him in French.'

"Does God speak as perfume or odors, voices, or a touch? No! But we can comprehend God in these ways. That is our interpretation of God's presence. Let us

22. Recording 468B: 1962 Chicago Closed Class, "Preparation for Prayer."

learn to accept God in whatever way and in whatever form God may appear to us. How do we know that it is God? How do we know that it is not imagination? By the fruitage, by the results. . . .

"When our experience is actually an experience of God, we can know it by its fruits, and the fruits of the spirit are joy, peace, prosperity, health, harmony, and love. When the Presence announces itself, there comes with it a sense of serenity, tranquility, a peace which may translate itself into form."[23]

As Joel said, prayer is an attitude and an altitude of consciousness. It is an attitude in which we are listening for impartations from God. God is always "broadcasting," always revealing Itself, and in this altitude of silence and receptivity, when we are truly in prayer, we can receive the divine messages.

"It is the nature of the sun to express light and warmth. Consequently, when we walk in the sunlight, we have no thought of *asking* for light and warmth—we merely accept them and enjoy them. The nature of God is love: therefore, there is no need to pray in terms of what we desire to receive from God. Simply entering into the Presence bestows the fullness of Life, Truth, Love— without taking thought, without asking, without praying for them. So think of yourself as walking out into the sunlight, being enfolded in its light and warmth. Think further of entering into communion with God, being enveloped and surrounded by the radiance of the Presence, in which the divine qualities and activities are revealed as the harmonies of your experience. For just as the sun expresses itself as light and warmth, so does

---

23. *Leave Your Nets:* Chapter 8: "Living the Life of Grace."

God express Itself as harmony, wholeness, completeness, perfection, dominion, power, joy, and peace."[24]

THE MEANING OF ANSWERED PRAYER

To those who practice the prayer of petition, "answered prayer"
means getting what you prayed for. But in The Infinite Way,
"answered prayer" has a different meaning. Joel taught that
answered prayer is hearing or experiencing some impartation
from within, in the silence of receptivity.

" Rightly understood, prayer is any attitude that opens
us to receptivity to God's grace. Answered prayer
comes only when there is an impartation from within to
our awareness—not when something goes out *from* us
to God, but when something comes *to* us from God."[25]

Impartations from within, or a sense of peace, or whatever
form in which we experience the Presence, is "answered prayer."
It is the "answer" to our "listening," our prayer of silence and receptivity. If we do not experience anything at the time that we
are meditating or praying, we might experience the effects of
our silent receptivity later. For example, some problem in our
life may be solved in a way that we did not expect. That, too, is
answered prayer. It is the activity of the Christ answering our
willingness to be still and listen.

" Answered prayer is the result of a divine impulse,
felt or sensed within. I'll repeat: Answered prayer
is the result of a divine impulse, felt or sensed within.

---

24. *The Heart of Mysticism: Volume 3, The 1956 Infinite Way Letters:* Chapter 3: March,
"The Part We Play."
25. *The Altitude of Prayer:* Chapter 1, "True Prayer, the Source of Our Good."

Then, you see, answered prayer has nothing to do with anything you do, but something you become aware of."[26]

So answered prayer is the spiritual impulse or impartation from within. At some point, that spiritual impulse may appear to us as a material form, but the material form is not the answered prayer. The spiritual impulse is.

Answered prayer comes when we have truly prayed, which means that we have prepared for prayer, that we are listening within in the attitude of receptivity, *and* that we have "fulfilled the terms of prayer."

Terms of prayer? What terms? Can't we just retire to a quiet place and pray? It depends. For prayer to be fruitful, there are conditions. Understanding these conditions and meeting them is another way in which prayer in The Infinite Way differs from much conventional prayer. Joel says:

"I'm sure you have wondered as many times as I have, why more prayer is not answered. Why, for so many centuries, people have been praying to God in every possible manner—standing, sitting, and lying down, fasting, and feasting—and why so few of these prayers are answered. And of course, the answer is this: prayer can never be answered unless there has been a fitting preparation for prayer *and* the terms of prayer are fulfilled—and there are terms. . . .

"One of these terms, of course, is humility. You will remember that he [Jesus] says if you approach the altar to pray and there remember that any man has ought against thee, first get up and make thy peace with thy brother and then return to the altar. Now, think how many times we have prayed without first making peace

---

26. Recording 97A: 1954 Portland Practitioner Class, "Our Real Identity and Oneness."

with our fellow man, and then you will understand one of the reasons that prayer is not answered.

"It is not possible for prayer to reach God through the mind or consciousness of an individual who is not at peace with his fellow man, and that means this: if there is anyone who has persecuted you or despitefully used you, harmed you, insulted you, there is a matter of forgiving even unto seventy times seven, and if you are carrying anyone in your mind unforgiven, your prayers are wasted. You cannot come to the throne of God except pure and humble in Spirit. You can, but it won't do any good so far as prayer is concerned. First there must be this humility that compels you to make peace with your fellow man.

"Now, it may well be that you have friends or relatives who will not make peace with you. That is not your problem. It doesn't mean that you are to compel them to be on good terms with you. It only means that you, in your heart, are bearing no grievance toward them— friends, relatives, or enemies. You yourself must be completely free of animosity, of any desire for revenge, of any unwillingness to forgive unto seventy times seven. This act of humility is demanded of you before there can be answered prayer."[27]

Furthermore, we must live in a spirit of forgiveness.

"Life must be a continuous forgiving. Day after day after day we have to remind ourselves, 'I hold no one in judgment, criticism, or condemnation. Not that I do not know the human faults of many; not that I condone

27. Recording 460A: 1962 Los Angeles Closed Class, "Maundy Thursday and Preparation for Prayer."

the acts of dictators or bosses; but that I can sincerely say, 'Father, forgive them, they know not what they do.'[28] I do not seek that they be revenged or avenged upon. I do not seek that they be overcome or destroyed, but rather that they be forgiven.'

"Think how many times since the days of the ancient prayers that we have prayed for the destruction of our enemies. This is a barrier to answered prayer. The moment you pray for the destruction of anyone's enemies, even your nation's enemies, you have cut yourself off from God. You cannot pray for the destruction of anyone. You may only pray that they be forgiven. You may only pray that their eyes be opened, their hearts be opened, their ears be opened, and that they may be forgiven their sins.

"This is prayer. This is an attitude of prayer, and this is a high altitude of prayer. You must rise high in consciousness, high in altitude, before you can really pray, 'Father, forgive these tyrants. Father, forgive these who have caused the world's destruction or who are causing what may be its destruction. Father, do not destroy them—forgive them. Open their eyes, open their ears, open their hearts.' Then you are in an attitude and an altitude of prayer in which you will find your prayers are answered. Harmony is being revealed in your experience."[29]

Humility, forgiveness, and loving thy neighbor as thy self, are the purifying influences that prepare the heart for true prayer and for answered prayer.

---

28. Luke 23:34.
29. Recording 468B: 1962 Chicago Closed Class, "Preparation for Prayer."

" There must be this openness of heart, this purity of motive that is willing to embrace the entire universe, and then without telling God our problem, without asking God's help, we become a transparency into which and through which the love of God can flow to the world of men, women, children, friends and enemies. . . . 'My heart is open to receive God's grace that it may flow to my neighbor—my friendly neighbor and my enemy neighbor, my nearby neighbor and my far away enemy.' In this purity of motive, you will find answered prayer."[30]

MEDITATION IS OUR MODE OF PRAYER

Joel gives us a new perspective on prayer. To summarize, in The Infinite Way, the whole nature of prayer is based on the nature of God as omniscience. Prayer is never an attempt to influence God, and if we pray *for* anything, we pray only for spiritual things. Prayer is listening, not speaking, and answered prayer is receiving a spiritual impulse or impartation within, in the silence of receptivity. These are significant and meaningful differences between prayer in The Infinite Way and the customary prayer of petition.

In The Infinite Way, the actual *practice* of prayer is also called meditation. Joel makes this clear when he says, "Meditation is our *mode* of prayer."[31] In other words, meditation is the way we pray. We can refer to the practice by either word—prayer or meditation—and Joel uses the words interchangeably. "You see, meditation is really prayer, and prayer is meditation."[32]

Once a student asked Joel, "Are the words 'praying' and 'meditating' synonymous?" He answered, "Virtually yes. . . .

30. Recording 460A: 1962 Los Angeles Closed Class, "Maundy Thursday and Preparation for Prayer."
31. *God, The Substance of All Form*: Chapter 2, "Building the New Consciousness."
32. *Living The Infinite Way*: Chapter 2, "Attaining the God-Experience."

On the whole, the way we use it in this literature, prayer and meditation are used synonymously."[33]

Regardless of what we call it, the important thing is to understand what prayer is and how to pray. Prayer, or meditation, is the primary practice in The Infinite Way, and we will address it in the next chapter, "Practices in The Infinite Way."

---

33. Recording 304B: 1960 Los Angeles Closed Class, "The 'I.'"

CHAPTER 8

PRACTICES IN THE INFINITE WAY

BY WORKING DILIGENTLY with the practices that Joel recommends, students can progress toward realizing the purpose of The Infinite Way message: "to become consciously aware of this divine Presence and to experience this Presence as the very Christ or Son of God within us, actually living our lives for us."[1] Just as one masters a musical instrument or becomes a great tennis player through dedicated practice, we make spiritual progress in proportion to our devotion to practice.

Joel teaches many practices in The Infinite Way, but these are at the core:

- Practicing the Presence
- Meditation, or prayer
- Studying Infinite Way writings and recordings
- Studying scripture
- Practicing the principles (nature of God, nature of individual being, nature of error, nature of prayer)
- Associating and communing with others on the path

---

1. *The Heart of Mysticism: Volume 5, The 1958 Infinite Way Letters*: Chapter 6: June, "Security Through God-Realization."

PRACTICING THE PRESENCE

The first practice that Joel recommends for new students is practicing the Presence. "Practice" means "to perform or work at repeatedly to become proficient," and practicing the Presence is "practice" in that sense. It means bringing our awareness to the presence of God, to spiritual truth, repeatedly and regularly throughout the day and the night, keeping thought on the omnipresence, omnipotence, and omniscience of God. Really, it is practicing the principle of the nature of God.

" $\mathbf{P}$ racticing the presence of God means that in any way and in every way, we shall consciously dwell on the idea of God, on some thought of God, on some aspect of God, on some spiritual teaching of God. God should be kept in the forefront of our consciousness. We have scripture that says, 'Thou wilt keep him in perfect peace, whose mind is stayed on Thee.'[2] That is practicing the presence of God. Keeping the mind stayed on God is practicing the presence of God. 'Acknowledge Him; lean not unto thine own understanding; acknowledge Him in all thy ways'[3]—that is practicing the presence of God.

"If you awaken in the morning and allow your first thought to be 'Thank you, Father, for having given us this light of day, and for having awakened me to it,' you have acknowledged God's presence. If at your breakfast table, you pause for a second, even if only to blink your eyes in recognition of the fact that God has set this table, and that God can set the table in the wilderness . . . you have acknowledged God in another way.

"If you go about household tasks, marketing, shop-

---

2. Isaiah 26:3.
3. See Proverbs 3:5-6.

ping, or business, and acknowledge that the presence of God is your wisdom, your strength, your guidance, you are again keeping your mind stayed on God. . . . Throughout your day, and throughout your evening, and throughout your night, you find an opportunity to acknowledge God's grace, to acknowledge God's presence, to acknowledge God's power, to acknowledge God's law operating in you and through you and upon you."[4]

Joel said, "A mind imbued with truth is a law of harmony unto our life,"[5] and by practicing the Presence, we are imbuing the mind with truth. Eventually, practicing the Presence becomes a way of life, and we do it automatically.

Practicing the Presence Is a Preparation for Meditation or Prayer

Joel recognized that some students had difficulty attaining the inner quiet and stillness required for meditation or prayer, and he realized that practicing the Presence could help bring about that stillness.

" Meditation is not simple for those who have never approached it. It is made easier, however, by beginning not with meditation itself, but with practicing the presence of God. It means consciously remembering God, acknowledging Him in all our ways . . . Gradually by this practice of the Presence, it becomes a simple matter to meditate because now, as we sit down, we au-

---

4. Recording 231A: 1958 London Open Class, "Practicing the Presence—Communion—Union."
5. *A Parenthesis in Eternity*: Chapter 18, "The Function of the Mind."

tomatically find ourselves in the midst of an inner quiet and an inner rhythm."[6]

"The question is asked, 'How do you learn to be still? How can you silence the human mind? How can you be quiet?' We have learned through the years that practicing the presence of God is the beginning of it, because it enables us to get quiet enough inside so that we can meditate."[7]

MEDITATION OR PRAYER

Joel said that meditation is the most important practice in The Infinite Way. Why? Because "The kingdom of God is within you,"[8] and to become consciously aware of the presence of God, you must go where it is to be found—within. But we are so bombarded with the thoughts, ideas, and opinions of "this world" that we have to remove ourselves from the noise and activity so that we can go within and experience the Presence.

"Meditation is the secret of this entire work. If you succeed in catching the vision of the Infinite Way, you will find that meditation will be responsible for at least ninety percent of that success. You will find that meditation is not only that which opens up consciousness, but meditation, ultimately, is the mode and means of bringing the Christ into manifestation. . . .

"The work of the Infinite Way is to reveal the kingdom of God within your own being. . . . But if I do not help you to attain the ability to meditate, you will not

---

6. *I Stand on Holy Ground:* Chapter 4, "The Stature of Spiritual Manhood."
7. Recording 283A: 1959 Lausanne Closed Class, "Practicing the Presence and Practicing Meditation."
8. Luke 17:21.

arrive at that final step of meeting God face to face. And that is what you must do. You have to find God; you have to meet God face to face."[9]

"Meditation takes your thought entirely away from the outside world and brings it within yourself where the kingdom of God is. Within yourself is where you will have to find God. Since a God experience is an activity of your consciousness and has to be experienced through your consciousness, when you are within yourself, within your own consciousness, you are at that point where the experience can take place, that is, where the demonstration of God takes place. It never takes place outside your being."[10]

Joel emphasized that studying and learning the letter of truth is not sufficient to attain the realized consciousness of God. Studying and learning are mental activities, and God cannot be experienced through the mind.

"Far too many aspirants to the spiritual way of life know the letter of truth and are satisfied to stop there. 'I and my Father are one' is the correct letter of truth. Does repeating these words or does an intellectual knowledge of them help us in any way? How often do we say: 'I am God's perfect child; I am spiritual; I am divine;' and then find that we are just as poor as we were before, or in just as much trouble? These are only statements. It is similar to sitting in a dark room and saying over and over again, 'Electricity gives light.' That is a correct statement, but we shall still be sitting in the

---

9. *The Master Speaks:* Chapter 15: "Meditation and Healing."
10. *Showing Forth the Presence of God*, Chapter 9, "Seek the Substance, Not the Form."

dark until, by turning on the switch, a connection is made with the source of electricity. So nothing is going to happen to us, regardless of how many affirmations of truth we know or repeat, unless we attain the consciousness of that truth and realize our oneness with our Source. Meditation is that way."[11]

Meditation is not an attempt to reach God, for God is already present. It is attaining such stillness that we can have the *conscious awareness* of that presence.

The Purpose of Meditation in The Infinite Way

There are many different forms of meditation, and they differ in their *purpose*. Some forms of meditation are for the purpose of relaxation, some for developing concentration, some for reducing stress, some for living a more mindful life, and some for simply attaining a state of peace. Joel was clear about the purpose of meditation in The Infinite Way:

"Meditation is not an end in itself. It is a means to an end. It is merely a vehicle through which we attain an awareness of the presence of God. There are some people who use meditation as an end in itself. All they want to do is to sit for an hour or two or three in the silence. Do not do that. Use meditation as a means to an end, as the means of being quiet for a moment to feel the presence of God, and that is all."[12]

"In and of itself, meditation is nothing. Meditation is an instrument *through* which we arrive somewhere, but meditation isn't the place we're going. The place

---

11. *Practicing the Presence*: Chapter 7, "Meditation."
12. *The Master Speaks*: Chapter 15: "Meditation and Healing."

we're going is conscious union with God. That's our goal; that's the attainment, and meditation is just *one* of the ways that we use."[13]

" The purpose of meditation and prayer is communion with the Father within you."[14]

" The purpose of meditation is not to heal, not to save, not to reform, not to redeem, not to enrich. The purpose of meditation is coming face-to-face with God, meeting God in the secret place of the Most High, which is within you."[15]

How to Meditate

Joel recommended a specific approach to meditation, which he describes in several books and classes. However, he said that you can use any method that works for you, as long as you understand that the purpose of meditation is to experience the presence of God, the Christ, within your own being. Joel's suggested form of meditation for beginners, as given in his books and classes, is summarized below.

The first step in meditation is to make yourself physically comfortable. Sit with your spine positioned comfortably, your feet on the floor, your hands relaxed in your lap. Breathe normally. There is no mystical or occult reason for this. It is simple: When the body is perfectly comfortable, one is not conscious of it, and one can be "absent from the body and present with the truth."[16] But the particular posture assumed is not important.

---

13. Recording 240A: 1958 First Maui Lectures: "The Message of The Infinite Way and Its Practice."
14. *Showing Forth the Presence of God*: Chapter 5, "God, the Substance of Universal Being."
15. Recording 147B: 1956 Second Steinway Hall Practitioner Class, "God Realization is Pure Demonstration."
16. See 2 Corinthians 5:8.

When you sit down to meditate or pray, sometimes you may not be able to find the deep silence right away. In that case, use "contemplative meditation" as a first step. Contemplative meditation is contemplating a spiritual question or quotation, and it helps you settle into quietness to prepare for meditation.

For example, you can ask yourself the question "What is God?" Probably you have some concept of what God is. But that concept could be someone else's concept, and now you are not interested in another's concept of God. You are only interested in asking, "What is God?" and receiving the answer from God. (If you are uncomfortable with the word God, use some other term that for you, refers to that invisible abiding Presence, the ultimate Source of Being.) The kingdom of God is within you, so the answer must come from within your own being. You are not trying to figure it out. Rather, you are letting the question float in your awareness and gently putting aside anything you think you know in order to allow something new to arrive.

Sit quietly with the attitude, "Speak to me, I am listening." Assume the feeling of waiting to hear a response. Relax and listen, as if you were waiting for a concert to begin for which you have no program and do not know what music will be played. Have no idea or expectation of what you might experience. Make it as effortless as you can.

As you listen, thoughts will come. Some thoughts may be about what God is. Contemplate whatever comes to you, and when the contemplation seems complete, return to the question "What is God?" When something else comes about God, contemplate that. You can go on for a year, or two or three, with the same question 'What is God?' and every time receive a different or deeper answer.

During your contemplative meditation, thoughts may come about your human situation—things you have to do or problems you have to solve—and your mind may want to engage those thoughts. If such thoughts come, do not fight them. Just let them come and let them go. Try not to engage them. Gently tell your-self: "I can think about that later. Right now, I am going to focus on the question 'What is God?'" Do not be upset at the intrusion of these thoughts. It is quite normal for this to occur, especially in the beginning. The mind is not accustomed to contemplating truth, and it will seek to return to the comfort zone of its normal activity—thinking and worrying about the practicalities of life. So be gentle and be patient. As you continue to practice medita-tion, interference from such thoughts will subside. Gently bring your mind back to the question "What is God?"

We may be engaged in mental activity, in thinking, during the contemplative meditation, but that serves the important purpose of bringing us into a receptive state and preparing us for the stillness and silence of true prayer or meditation. Then the presence of God can come into our experience.

At some point your contemplative meditation will stop, and you move into a higher form of meditation.

"Someday . . . you will suddenly find that you cannot think any more; you have come to the end of thought about God. Then you will sit quietly at peace—no more thoughts, no more questions, no more answers; just peace and listening. The real meditation is just listening. All the rest is for the purpose of arriving at that point of listening. When you are listening, you are meditating. The whole object of meditation is opening consciousness. You do not have to experience any occult phenomena.

"Thought will be quieted, the inner ear will open, and a long deep breath, like a sigh of relief or a sense of release, may come to you. It is as if a burden were drop-ping off your shoulders. It can appear in many different ways, but when that release comes, you will be filled with the Spirit. There will be an inner alertness. With that release will come divine wisdom, divine guidance, and divine strength because that deep breath, that 'click,' or release, was a God-experience—the actual presence or activity of God in your consciousness."[17]

" We must never forget that this God to whom we are praying, to whom we are attuning ourselves, is within us. We are not thinking up to heaven; we are not thinking out into the world; we are attuned to the center of our own being from which the grace of God flows."[18]

Joel encouraged students to have patience with their progress, because learning to meditate takes time and practice. One of the best ways to fully understand meditation as practiced in The Infinite Way is to read Joel's book *The Art of Meditation*, which addresses all aspects of meditation. In the book, Joel gives instructions about how to meditate and how to handle difficulties that might arise. He describes the stages of meditation, and he elaborates on the fruits of meditation practice.

STUDYING THE INFINITE WAY WRITINGS AND RECORDINGS

A third core practice in The Infinite Way is studying the writings and recordings. Joel emphasized that the experience of God usually does not come without a firm foundation in the correct letter of truth, and that meditation itself must be backed up with an understanding of the spiritual principles. Studying The Infinite Way writings and recordings give us that foundation in the correct letter of truth.

---

17. *Living The Infinite Way*: Chapter 2, "Attaining the God-Experience."
18. *The Art of Spiritual Living*: Chapter 5, "The New Dispensation of Prayer."

"In the early stages of the development of spiritual consciousness, you fill yourself with truth by reading, by listening to recordings and attending tape recording meetings, by individual study with a teacher who has gone a step beyond you, and by attendance at classes. The more inspirational literature you read, the more classes you attend, and the more recordings you hear, the more does your thought become spiritualized, and the clearer transparency for truth do you become."[19]

"The Bible, the writings of The Infinite Way, the tape recordings, the tape recording meetings, and the class work, if properly utilized, serve a twofold purpose. First, these implant the letter of truth in the mind and then [second] they become the instruments by which truth becomes conscious awareness, a feeling in the heart."[20]

"Without the attainment of the knowledge of the correct letter of truth and its proof in your experience, it is almost impossible to attain the spirit of truth, the actual consciousness of truth, which is the 'My kingdom'—the spiritual kingdom, or consciousness."[21]

Yet Joel always reminded students that these study resources were just instruments in the service of a higher goal.

---

19. *The Heart of Mysticism: Volume 5, The 1958 Infinite Way Letters:* Chapter 1: January, "Spiritual Unfoldment Through the Study of The Infinite Way."
20. ibid.
21. *The Heart of Mysticism: Volume 5, The 1958 Infinite Way Letters:* Chapter 10: October 1958 Letter, "Break the Fetters that Bind You."

"The Infinite Way is not its writings. The Infinite Way is not its recordings, or let's put it the other way: The writings do not constitute The Infinite Way nor do the recordings, nor the classes. The writings, recordings, classes are instruments leading us to The Infinite Way, and The Infinite Way itself is a God experience."[22]

"It is not the books that do it; it is not the tape recordings of my classes that do it; it is not the classes: it is the consciousness that is built by means of the books, the tapes, and the classes. That is why all these adjuncts are helpful to us, not because they have any value in and of themselves. The value is in the consciousness they develop."[23]

"The whole aim of every one of these books is to send you back into the kingdom of God, not tell you something I've discovered. Those are just little helps on the way. You don't have to take one single thing that I've discovered as a truth. You don't have to. Just take the overall intent of the books to drive you back through meditation, contemplation, into your own withinness and be taught of God. And I don't mind if you throw the books out the window or give them away to somebody not yet that far advanced. This isn't a teaching that says, 'I have the truth that will make you free.' Oh, no. This is a teaching that says, 'The kingdom of God is within you, and if I can get you back there, *it* will reveal to you the truth that will make you free.'"[24]

---

22. Recording 20B: 1953 New Hawaiian Series, "God as Law in Operation, continued."
23. *The Art of Spiritual Living*: Chapter 4, "The Hidden Kingdom."
24. Recording 643A: 1956 Johannesburg Closed Class, "The Anointed of God."

Lorraine Sinkler said, "Joel did not believe in believing. . . . The principles he set forth were the direct result of inner revelation and unfoldment which he had proved to be true in his years of healing work, but which he did not regard as sufficient reason for anyone else's acceptance of them. In The Infinite Way nobody is an authority; nobody has to be accepted, believed, or followed."[25] She said that Joel never encouraged students to lean on him, but always turned them to a reliance on their own consciousness. Joel himself said:

"I have but one wish for the students of The Infinite Way, and all others on the Path, and that is, not that they accept what my experience in and with God has been, but that each one may himself experience God, know God, feel God, love and understand God, and finally realize Godhood."[26]

"Many words of the Infinite Way message have been printed, and many, many more have been recorded on tape, but all of these have but one purpose: to drive us back into that kingdom within our own being, to drive us to that level of consciousness where Truth imparts Itself to us. Every word that has been spoken or written in this message has had but one intent: to lift consciousness into an atmosphere where we may individually receive the impartation of Truth."[27]

Even when we do receive impartations or revelations from within, it can take a while to fully absorb them. As Joel said:

25. Sinkler, Lorraine, *The Spiritual Journey of Joel Goldsmith*, Chapter 9, "Building for Eternity."
26. *Living The Infinite Way:* Chapter 4, "God Is One."
27. *Spiritual Discernment:* Chapter 2: "God Must Be an Experience, Not a Concept."

"Regardless of how many revelations I have had, I have not been able immediately to demonstrate them. It has taken time for it to settle in my consciousness and become a demonstrable principle. I see the principle; I catch it. But it is so contrary to everything that I've ever humanly learned that it takes time to assimilate it, and it takes even a little more time before it begins to flow naturally."[28]

A Plan for Studying the Books and Recordings

Chapter 11 of this book presents a suggested plan for embarking on a study of The Infinite Way message.

STUDYING SCRIPTURE

"Every message that is in the Infinite Way writings is a message based on some passage of scripture, some incident or some story of scripture, but brought alive by the inspiration and the revelation that have been given to me on the subject."[29]

Studying scripture is another practice that Joel encouraged. He said that if we work attentively with passages from scripture, it is possible to be in the consciousness of those who received those revelations and wrote them down, and to grasp their original meaning.

Once again, Joel cautioned that the Bible and the truths of the Bible will not do anything for us in a book. We must take them into our consciousness and ponder them, as if they were seeds that we were planting.

---

28. Recording 175A: 1956 New York Laurelton Hotel Closed Class, "I Say Unto You."
29. *Living by the Word*: Chapter 8: "Scripture As a Way of Life."

" There is no better way to begin the development of spiritual consciousness than with a study of the Bible. The Bible is a great historical document and, as a piece of literature, it ranks among the greatest because of its beauty of expression. It is not for such reasons that we read it, however, because for us, the Bible embodies a great spiritual teaching; it is a guide which can lead us in the way everlasting. We may find the historical and literary aspects of the Bible interesting, but our real interest is in the Bible as a way of life."[30]

In the book *Spiritual Interpretation of Scripture*, Joel said that the Bible is not just a history of events that took place thousands of years ago. He says, "Scripture is the unfolding of characters and movements or happenings that are taking place within you—right this minute. Every Biblical experience can be found in your consciousness at some time or other."[31] In other words, we embody within ourselves every Bible of the world, every philosophy, character, and story, and when these are interpreted spiritually, they can be understood as states and stages of our own spiritual development and unfoldment.

Joel recommended several ways to work with Scripture. For example,

" Now, the best approach is this: you meditate—you may even have the Bible in your hands—and you meditate, and you turn within:

Father, I'm seeking Thy word. Father, I'm seeking the kingdom of God, the realm of God. I'm seeking

---

30. *The Heart of Mysticism: Volume 5, The 1958 Infinite Way Letters:* Chapter 1: January, "Spiritual Unfoldment Through the Study of The Infinite Way."
31. *Spiritual Interpretation of Scripture:* "Darkness to Light."

that word of life which is life eternal. I'm seeking Thy word. I know man shall not live by bread alone, but by every word that proceedeth out of the mouth of God. I know that in this book there are spiritual saints and seers and sages, leaders, saviors, all who have been divinely inspired. They have written in this book the word of life . . . and I'm going to open it. Father, instruct me. Father, give me light on this volume. Father, lead me back to the very consciousness of your saints and sages and seers who wrote in this book. Let me see the vision they saw. Let me hear the words they heard. Give me the message that they meant to convey.

"Then you are still for a few moments, and you open your Bible. What your experience will be, I don't know in the beginning. But I know that if you persist in this, the day will come when you will open your Bible, and things will stand out there as if they were in electric lights, and hidden meanings will reveal themselves to you."[32]

Scripture study changed the experience of many of Joel's students, and he could see the benefits:

"In the past thirty years I have watched hundreds of people who have come out of ordinary life, with no more knowledge of scripture than they were able to pick up by attending a church service or something of that kind, and after they began to live with scripture and to make the passages of scripture a part of their everyday living, I have seen the change in their nature, in their character, in their lives, in their health, and in their

---

32. Recording 383A: 1960 Auckland Closed Class, "Healing Principles of The Infinite Way."

supply. I have watched a complete change in human relationships the very moment that scripture became a living word to them. . . .

"When we study and search the scriptures, we are fed as we never before have been fed; we are guided, directed, protected as we never before have been; but always in direct proportion as we make these passages of scripture our daily bread."[33]

PRACTICING THE PRINCIPLES

We said that The Infinite Way is a teaching, a way of life, and an experience. When we considered The Infinite Way as a teaching, we focused on the four major principles in the teaching—the nature of God, the nature of individual being, the nature of error, and the nature of prayer. Once we understand those principles, we can practice them in daily living so that the teaching becomes a way of life.

" The young student—the beginning student—should realize that there are specific principles that constitute the message of The Infinite Way. If these principles are not understood and *practiced*, The Infinite Way remains in the category of a philosophy, just an interesting approach to life, something to read about and then put on a shelf. But that is in no sense what The Infinite Way is. The Infinite Way is a living experience, practical for use in everyday life."[34]

Joel constantly reminded students that learning the principles, or what he called "the correct letter of truth" is necessary

---

33. *Living by the Word*: Chapter 8, "Scripture as a Way of Life."
34. *The Contemplative Life*: Chapter 9, "Daily Preparation for Spiritual Living."

to build a foundation for spiritual living. But he knew that intellectual acceptance and understanding alone would never change anyone's experience. To prove the principles for ourselves and gain the *realized* consciousness of truth, we must put the principles into practice. Again and again, Joel said that practicing the principles is what separates those who make progress on the spiritual path from those who do not.

" The Infinite Way is a way of life, but it is not a way that can be accomplished through reading or hearing. It can only be accomplished by using the readings, the writings, the hearings as a means toward another end, and that other end is *practicing the message* until it becomes a *way of life* within one."[35]

" This is no different from taking piano lessons or any other kind of lessons. You go to your teacher and take a lesson, but if you do not practice, you will receive no benefit from another lesson the next day. In the same way, your unfoldment, understanding, and progress in truth will be in the degree of your putting each and every one of these lessons into practice."[36]

How Do We Practice the Principles?

Joel gives many lessons on how to practice the principles. For example, here he explains how to practice the principle of the nature of individual being with respect to oneself.

" We must learn through constant effort to get close to the 'I' that I am. A hundred times a day some suggestion will come about our human selfhood, and a

---

35. Recording 65B: 1954 Honolulu Lecture Series, "Meditation on One Power."
36. *Conscious Union with God:* "Introduction."

hundred and one times we must meet this suggestion with the conscious understanding and declaration that only that which is infinite, eternal, spiritual is true of us, of our true selfhood, and naught else can 'enter to defile.' For weeks, perhaps for months, we must watch what enters thought so that nothing is accepted as our true identity that is not true of God. Gradually we will become accustomed to thinking from the standpoint of perfect selfhood, in which case we cannot have a sense of 'I am sick' or 'I am lonesome' or 'I am discouraged' because the selfhood that can be these things has been renounced so that it is no longer a part of consciousness. Whatever of sin, sickness or limitation had been a part of the human concept of ourselves has gone into nothingness with the material selfhood, and that which is true, eternal, immortal of the 'I' that I now recognize myself to be, is the only manifestation and expression.

"This is not a lazy man's work. It requires many weeks of conscious effort to separate the false sense of self with its beliefs of limitations from the real Self, the only 'I' that I am, until only the spiritual selfhood talks and hears—voices only truth, and hears only 'a still, small voice.'"[37]

As another example, Joel explains how we practice the principle of the nature of individual being with respect to others:

" God constitutes individual being. This means God is the life of every individual—God is the mind, God is the soul, God is the spirit, God is the law, and even one's body is the temple of God. God constitutes individual being. God is the essence, the substance, the

---

37. *The Early Years:* Chapter 5, "True Identity."

law, and the life of individual being, and therefore the nature of man is godly, or good.

"Now of course, this is not going to be difficult for you when you are looking around at a group of serious, studious, metaphysicians.... Your difficulty in practicing this will be when you walk out on the street and somebody pushes you off in their haste to get by, or somebody comes down the street intoxicated or using obscene language, or when you witness somebody profiting by their thefts and dishonesties, or when you read the news of the police courts each day.... Then it is going to be a very difficult thing for you to agree with this principle.

"And then it is that you are going to have your hard, hard, work, because you will have to close your eyes and look through the appearance and agree that even though appearances do not testify to this, this must be the truth, because God made all that was made, and all that God made is good. Anything that God did not make was not made. Therefore, it must be literally true that God is the substance of all being, the substance of all form, the substance of individual being, the life and the law of individual being.

"And so begins the period of discipleship, when you are practicing this principle with appearances against you. Oh yes, even in the circle of your own home and your friends and your relatives, you are very often going to find it difficult to believe that this is true—that the nature of man is godly. And yet, in spite of these appearances, in spite of bad conduct, in spite of sin, in spite of failings, there is no other way but to obey this law and stand in this truth: God constitutes individual being and the nature of man is godly.

"Soon enough you'll see how difficult this is and why it is a discipline to stand in a truth like this, but the miracle is that eventually, these very people who have been acting badly toward you or in your presence, the very people who seem to be in many ways unlike this godly nature, they begin to change in their attitude toward you. You now begin to behold that they are more nearly like what you have been declaring."[38]

Before we can practice the principles, we must know what the principles are. Then we can call them to mind and stand firm in them whenever we experience anything that seems to contradict them. In this example, Joel illustrates how we can practice the principle of the nature of error.

"When confronted with any form of error, it is often wise to ponder this passage of Scripture: 'My glory will I not give to another.'[39] God does not give Its power, substance, law, or activity to any form of sin, disease, or limitation. Think of the tremendous meaning here: No form of discord has power, activity, or law. No mortal concept, belief, or theory is spiritually endowed. . . .

"However, even after you have heard this and even after you believe it, it will only be a few hours before you will be tempted to disbelieve it or mistrust it—just long enough to hear a radio broadcast or read a newspaper headline. Then all of the truth is forgotten unless you are alert and have been willing to discipline yourself through study and by practice, so that you are instant

---

38. Recording 281B: 1959 England Open Class, "Practicing Presence, Meditation, and Treatment."
39. Isaiah 42:8.

in answering every suggestion and every appearance of evil with a conscious rebuke.

"In your present state of development, it is necessary to recognize that every bit of evil presented to you in the world is suggestion or appearance. It may well be that, because of the press of circumstances, you may be unable to stand fast in not accepting it into consciousness as a reality. In such situations, you would be wise to turn within and remind yourself of some truth: 'What is this that is coming to me? Do I have to believe it? Why should I believe anything apart from God? God made all that was made, and all that God made was good. Anything God did not make was not made, and so this that is coming to me was never made. It has no reality; it has no substance, law, cause, or effect; and therefore, I do not have to believe it or accept it into my consciousness.' . . .

"All you have done is to clear your own consciousness so that you do not accept the appearance as reality. Then you must become very still, 'Speak, Lord; for thy servant heareth,'[40] and in that listening attitude make your conscious contact with God. Only when consciousness is opened to God is God made available.

"Until you become convinced that the only power there is, is within your own being, you will be under the necessity of mentally disciplining yourself every time you come up against an appearance. Thus you will be building spiritual consciousness. Spiritual consciousness is your consciousness when there is a complete confidence in the Infinite Invisible."[41]

---

40. 1 Samuel 3:10.

41. *The Heart of Mysticism: Volume 5, The 1958 Infinite Way Letters:* Chapter 1: January, "Spiritual Unfoldment Through the Study of The Infinite Way."

In other words, to practice the principle of the nature of error, which is based on God as omnipotence, we take refuge in the principle itself. "You should face every situation in life from the standpoint that no situation has any power. Since God is the only power, disease can have no power, sin can have no power, fear can have no power: there is no power but God."[42]

Joel said that practice was so important that even he had to practice the principles continuously.

"The benefit that students can get from my thirty years is not in reading my books or hearing my tape recordings but in *taking these principles of life and embodying them in their consciousness.*

"If I had not had to do the same thing, I would not tell students to do it. I have to keep it up as much as anyone else. I have to live morning, noon, and night in the conscious remembrance of these truths. I cannot let days go by, not even one day, not even an hour go by, without an activity of truth in my consciousness. I cannot answer my mail without turning, with every few letters, to that Spirit within for more light, more spirit, more and deeper awareness. And I know that no one else can either."[43]

When we practice the principles, we are not trying to *make* them true. The principles are already true, and we are simply choosing to hold to that truth. Practicing the principles should not be tiring; ideally, it will become effortless.

There is a story about a tourist in New York City who asked a native, "How do I get to Carnegie Hall?" The native answered,

---

42. *The Journey Back to the Father's House:* Chapter 2, "Letting the Seed Take Root."
43. *The Art of Spiritual Living:* Chapter 6, "Demands of the Spiritual Life."

"Practice, practice, practice." If we want to live in Christ-consciousness, we too must practice, practice, practice.

ASSOCIATING WITH OTHERS ON THE PATH

Joel taught another beneficial practice: associating and communing with others on the path. Being with like-minded individuals helps us stay centered in truth, and we are less likely to be tempted to discuss or accept the illusions and appearances in human life. Further, if we associate with others who have gone a step further on the path than we have, they can lift us, at least temporarily, to their level of consciousness.

" The Christ is always present with us; the Christ is the reality of our being; but the need is for the *conscious awareness* of the presence of the Christ. We develop that through studying and hearing the Word, coming together with other students on the path, and the revelation within our own being, brought about through meditation. Reading, association with others on the path, and meditation bring us to that state of consciousness where all of a sudden, the inner realization comes, and the Christ unfolds and discloses Its glory to us."[44]

" The reading of books and the study of Scripture is the first step of the way by which we open our consciousness to the inflow of spiritual Truth. The second step is *our association with those who are on the path*, and especially with those who have gone even one step further than we have."[45]

---

44. *The Master Speaks:* Chapter 2, "Reality of Spirit."
45. *The Master Speaks:* Chapter 1, "Oneness with God."

" S piritual consciousness is contagious: it is impossible to be in the presence of those who are making even the slightest degree of effort towards this awareness, without imbibing some of it from them."[46]

OTHER PRACTICES

This chapter focused on the major practices that Joel recommended. There are others, too, and if you choose to study The Infinite Way further, you will learn about them as you work with the books and recordings.

---

46. *Spiritual Interpretation of Scripture*: "Scriptural Symbols."

CHAPTER 9

SPIRITUAL HEALING

JOEL GOLDSMITH HAD an extraordinary spiritual healing ministry as well as a teaching ministry. He was known worldwide as a superbly successful spiritual healing practitioner, and many of his students became spiritual healing practitioners. While spiritual healing benefitted many individuals personally, Joel said that spiritual healing was important not because of the personal healings, but because spiritual healing proved the principles of The Infinite Way. "Healing work," he said, "is the proof of our work and of the rightness of the message."[1]

"Healing is the *proof* of whether or not this message, or any message, is true. . . . If it is true, it is resulting in harmony and peace, in joy and prosperity, in health and wholeness, at least in some measure in your individual experience and in the experience of those turning to you for help. That is your proof that the message is true."[2]

---

1. *The Master Speaks:* Chapter 10, "Spiritual Existence."
2. *God, The Substance of All Form:* Chapter 12, "Good Unfolding as the Activity of Individual Consciousness."

WHAT IS SPIRITUAL HEALING IN THE INFINITE WAY?

The term "spiritual healing" can refer to many different types of healing. To understand what is meant, we must know who is using the term and how they are using it. In The Infinite Way, spiritual healing has a specific meaning that is different from that in other teachings.

"As you come to the message of The Infinite Way, you also hear that term, 'spiritual healing.' We mean something far different than many of those other teachings because the spiritual healing of which we speak is a healing based on certain specific principles—principles of The Infinite Way. We have no more right to the term 'spiritual healing' than these others, and yet we have the same right that they have. But don't be misled into believing that all metaphysical healing or all healing that is not physical is spiritual healing according to the principles of The Infinite Way. If you wish to avail yourselves of Infinite Way healing, you must understand the principles upon which it is based and not try to bring into it principles which you may have learned in some other metaphysical teaching. . . .

"Remember that this does not mean right or wrong. This is in no wise saying that The Infinite Way healing method is right, and the others are wrong. This is definitely saying that Infinite Way healing principles *differ* from those of any other metaphysical teaching."[3]

---

3. Recording 261B: 1959 Hawaiian Village Open Class, "The Nature of Error."

Spiritual Healing Is Not About Changing the Picture

Joel could not have been more emphatic that in The Infinite Way, *spiritual healing is not about changing the human picture.* It is not a focused mental activity by which we try to overcome some error. In The Infinite Way, the spiritual healing practitioner never tries to influence God to do something, never fights an appearance, never tries to change a condition.

Just as one does not try to change 2 x 2 = 5, or remove the illusion of water on the desert, or try to straighten out the railroad tracks that seem to come together, the practitioner does not try to change an appearance. The practitioner recognizes that the appearance is an illusion, dismisses it, and rises in consciousness to the eternal perfection and harmony of Being. In other words, in spiritual healing, the practitioner does not try to meet the problem on the level of the problem.

Rather, as Joel says, "We go right to the center of being, and there recognize Christ, the Spirit, the presence and power of God. As we do that, we do not heal human beings; we do not enrich them, although that is the way in which it appears to the world. What we do is to bring to light their spiritual identity— that which has always been there, but which has seemed to have disappeared."[4] In other words, that which has obscured the truth is dispelled, just as when clouds disperse, the sun is revealed. The sun is always shining, but it can be hidden by clouds. Spiritual identity is always the reality of an individual, but it can be concealed by ignorance, misperceptions, and erroneous beliefs.

For a moment, go back to the principles of the nature of God, the nature of individual being, and the nature of error. If you accept those principles, could there be any discord or inharmony such as sin, disease, lack, or limitation? When we considered how to practice the principle of the nature of error, we said

---

4. *The Master Speaks:* Chapter 1, "Oneness with God."

that whenever there is an *appearance* of discord or limitation, we stand fast in the truth that since God is infinite and omnipotent, there can be no such thing as discord. We said that as we continue to hold that truth in consciousness, the discordant appearance dissolves. The "clouds" pass and the sunshine of truth beams forth. In the case of disease, the appearance dissolves, and the individual stands revealed in his native perfect harmony; revealed as the expression of the Divine that in truth, he *already* is. That is why in The Infinite Way, we say that "healing is revealing." Spiritual healing dispels the illusion and reveals the universe of perfection and harmony that already IS.

If we fight the problem or try to change the picture, we are acknowledging that there is something to fight, and there is not. So "healing is revealing" means that healing is the revealing, or appearing, of the truth where the error *seemed* to be. The "revealing" is the result of the practitioner taking no thought, seeking first the kingdom of God, and resting in the *realized consciousness* that health and harmony in their fullness are *already* in the nature of the patient's true spiritual identity.

THE BASIS FOR SPIRITUAL HEALING IN THE INFINITE WAY

The specific principles that underlie spiritual healing in The Infinite Way are the very principles that we have covered in the previous chapters. A spiritual healing practitioner is one who has attained the realized consciousness of these principles. Sometimes when Joel speaks about healing, he refers to these principles as "the healing principles," but he is referring to the same principles that we have discussed.

" Successful [healing] practitioners stand on the two basic principles: the nature of God and My kingdom, and the nature of evil and its world of illusion. They stand fast in those principles until they develop the consciousness that is not fooled by appearances."[5]

The Nature of God as a Healing Principle

Speaking of the nature of God as a healing principle, Joel says:

" To understand the nature of God is to understand the basic principle of spiritual healing. Is it the nature of God to heal disease? Do you really believe that? If God is all-powerful and all-loving, why did He not heal it yesterday? Why is He waiting for today? And why is He not doing it today? . . .

"God never has had pleasure in our dying; God never will have pleasure in our dying; and, furthermore, God has never been responsible for our dying. . . .When you understand God to be infinite love, infinite wisdom, and infinite good, you will know that God is 'of purer eyes than to behold evil, and canst not look on iniquity.'[6] . . . Through prayer and contemplation, let the nature of God be revealed. Discover for yourself that God has never empowered a disease to kill; God has never ordained a disease to destroy; and because of the all-loving nature of God, disease must be outside the creative, maintaining, and sustaining power of God, which means that it is without cause, without foundation, law, substance, or action. . . .

"When this reveals itself to you, never again will you appeal to God to overcome error in any form; never will you turn to truth to overcome error; never will you use right thinking to offset wrong thinking; never will you pray to God to heal disease, sin, or fear: You will know

---

5. *A Message for the Ages*: Chapter 9, "The Simplicity of the Healing Truth."
6. Habakkuk 1:13.

that in the infinite nature of God's goodness, disease, sin, and fear do not exist as power. In God's kingdom, there is no such thing as truth *over* error, God *over* the devil, good *over* evil, right *over* wrong, or Spirit *over* matter: *There is only infinite, immortal, eternal God-being."*[7]

The Nature of Error as a Healing Principle

Joel had this to say about the nature of error as a healing principle:

" The message of the Infinite Way has as its major healing principle the nature of error. If you can grasp the truth that all error, regardless of whether it is individual or collective, whether it concerns a person or a tidal wave, is actually nothing but the universal belief in two powers, you are a good practitioner and you will have excellent results. That has always been its principle, and still there are very few successful practitioners. Why? Because the belief in two powers is so firmly implanted in human consciousness that we are not able to look at a form of error and say, 'It is neither good nor evil.' We are determined to get rid of it, overcome it, or rise above it, or we are determined to try to get the power of God to do something to it.

"To be a teacher or practitioner of the Infinite Way does not mean that you have power to heal people of disease, of lack, or of discordant relationships. It means that you have attained the recognition of the *illusory* nature of what is presented to you as a problem. It does not mean that you are so close to God that God, through you, will do something for mankind. Heaven forbid that

---

7. *The Art of Spiritual Healing:* Chapter 3, "One Power."

God should be so localized as to be personal to anybody. To be a teacher, to be a practitioner, or to be able to help those who come to you means that you have attained an awareness of the principles of the Infinite Way and that through constantly living with them, studying them, and putting them into practice, your consciousness has evolved to that place where, when you are asked for help, you, too, can say, 'illusion.' . . .

"The kingdom of God is intact. Spiritual man has not degenerated into a mortal, and mortal man is never going to be lifted up into the status of a spiritual being. What happens is that the teacher or practitioner has attained the capacity to *see the spiritual son of God and not believe the appearance*, whether it testifies to sin, disease, lack, or limitation. This is a spiritual healer, not the one who prays to God that you be healed. The spiritual healer can look you right in the eye and say, 'I know who you are. You are God, Itself, individualized.' And then, to this appearance of sin, disease, false appetite, or lack, be able to say, 'That is the illusion: that is what would fool me into trying to do something to nothing.'"[8]

As you may recall from the chapter on the nature of error, the root of the discordant appearances is what Joel calls "hypnotism," or believing the appearance, and he tells us how to deal with it:

"A most important point to remember is that you do not get rid of hypnotism any more than you get rid of rheumatism. You do not overcome hypnotism; you do not struggle with it; you do not look for a God-power to do something to it. You merely recognize that the

---

8. *A Message for the Ages*: Chapter 6, "Not Appearances but Is."

substance or the fabric of this world is hypnotism and then drop it.

"If you were to see 2 x 2 = 5 on a paper or blackboard, you would not struggle to overcome it. You would merely say 2 x 2 = 4, and that is that. Or, you might say, 'That's a mistake.' But you would not do anything after you recognize it as a mistake because there is nothing to be done. Once you know it is a mistake, it does not fool you anymore.

"If somebody tells you a lie and you think it is the truth, you can get into trouble. But if someone tells you a lie and you know it is a lie, do you have to do anything? You don't even have to correct the liar, do you? Because you don't care what he is doing. That is his business. All you have to know is, 'That's a lie. I can't be fooled.' Right?

"If then a claim of any nature is presented to you and you recognize, 'That is neither person, place, nor thing. That is a state of hypnotism,' that's all you have to do. You are not fooled by it. You recognize it as a lie, and it has lost its power."[9]

"Remember, you are dealing with an appearance—an appearance produced by this universal malpractice, universal ignorance, universal hypnotism, believing in two powers—but only an appearance, and you are not to get rid of the appearance. You can't any more get rid of an appearance than you can get rid of the mirage on the desert. You can only see through it, and understand it to be a mirage, and then go on about your business. . . .

"The consciousness that does not respond to appearances is the healing consciousness. The consciousness that is aware of the spiritual nature of creation,

---

9. *A Message for the Ages:* Chapter 9, "The Simplicity of the Healing Truth."

and of the illusory nature of appearances, is a healing consciousness."[10]

Joel reminds us that we encounter appearances every day, but we don't react to them. We see railroad tracks come together, water on the road in a desert, the sky sitting on the mountain. We see the sun go across the sky and a moon that changes shape. But we are so accustomed to dismissing these illusions that we hardly notice them. To have the healing consciousness, we must get to that same place with the appearances of discord.

The Nature of Individual Being as a Healing Principle

In many classes, Joel adds that the nature of individual being is an important healing principle.

"God appearing as individual being—God appearing as you—is a secret of The Infinite Way; it is a secret of spiritual healing. This 'you' is not a reflection, or a separate idea, or something less than God, but God, Itself, made manifest—God, the Father, appearing on earth as individual Being. Oneness is the secret.

"After you have assimilated this truth by living with it, by practicing it, by looking out at every man, woman, and child, every animal, vegetable, and mineral in the world, and realizing, 'This is not what it seems to be: This is God appearing as,' you develop that healing consciousness which never looks at people and judges them by their humanhood, but which is immediately in contact with their spiritual consciousness. You train yourself to see people, not as they look, but to see through their eyes, back of their eyes, realizing that there sits the

10. Recording 477B: 1962 Princess Kaiulani Open Class, "Infinite Way Healing Principles."

Christ of God. As you do that, you learn to ignore appearances, and instead of trying to heal or reform someone, or improve him, you are really bearing witness to his Christ-identity. . . . If it is true that God manifests as individual being, then harmony already is the truth about every person."[11]

The Nature of Prayer as a Healing Principle

The principle of the nature of prayer comes into healing work, too. Healing is brought about in the silent, receptive consciousness of listening prayer. If the practitioner cannot rise immediately into a prayerful state, he or she might begin with a contemplative meditation. In healing work, Joel refers to these contemplative meditations as "treatment." The purpose of the treatment is simply to remind us of the truth and lift us to a state in which we can be in silent, receptive meditation, or prayer, and let divine Consciousness do the work. In other words, we can think of treatment as "treating" ourselves to the truth. It is a stepping-stone to prayer.

" Treatment is the truth that you and I know, the truth that we think, declare, or affirm in contradistinction to the error that is appearing. In other words, when I say that God is the law and the reality of my being, that God is my life, my Soul; when I say that God, the life which is God, is the eternality and immortality of my being; when I say that Christ is the law unto my being, and there is not a material law to act upon me; when I declare or affirm my oneness with God; when I declare or affirm the nothingness, the nonreality, of any form of error, that is treatment. In some metaphysical teach-

---

11. *The Art of Spiritual Healing*: Chapter 4: "The Language of Spiritual Healing."

ings, this would be considered prayer, but not in our work.

"In the Infinite Way, affirmations and denials have not been entirely eliminated. We do not do away completely with affirmations and denials, but we do not think of them as prayer; they are treatment, a statement or restatement of truth within our own thought. The purpose of the treatment is to remind ourselves of the truth of being, thereby lifting ourselves to that place where prayer is possible."[12]

THE MEANING OF A "HEALING CONSCIOUSNESS"

A practitioner who has a healing consciousness has developed a realized consciousness of the principles of the nature of God, the nature of individual being, the nature of error, and the nature of prayer. Statements of truth do not heal, and an intellectual knowledge of these principles is only a foundation. The healing agency is in the practitioner's degree of illumined, or realized, consciousness of the principles. Yet Joel always reminded us of the importance of building the foundation for that realized consciousness by working steadfastly with the principles.

" Do not believe for a moment that you can avoid those first years of specific application of specific truths in treatment, for this is what develops consciousness. Through the correct letter of truth, the spiritual awareness of truth is attained. ... [Developing a healing consciousness] means work, it requires diligence, and it demands of you perseverance. The important

---

12. *The Master Speaks:* Chapter 11, "The Allness of God."

thing is the amount of actual practice which you give to this work."[13]

Joel said that the most successful practitioners are the ones who know the principles exactly and thoroughly and do not deviate from them. As we learn and practice the principles, we are developing a healing consciousness, and when we have that realized consciousness of the principles, we have the healing consciousness, a consciousness that does not react to appearances and neither loves, hates, nor fears error.

HOW DOES SPIRITUAL HEALING WORK?

The Infinite Way teaches that when someone seeks healing help from a practitioner, they bring themselves not to the practitioner as a person, but to the realized God-consciousness of the practitioner. Then, the realized consciousness of the practitioner becomes the law unto the patient. "And I, if I be lifted up from the earth [from material consciousness], will draw all men unto me."[14] The practitioner's elevated consciousness lifts the consciousness of the one seeking help, and that uplifted consciousness of the patient shows forth as harmonious conditions.

" As you enter [the consciousness of the practitioner], that light, which is their knowledge of one power, their knowledge of one presence, their awareness of spiritual reality, this becomes the law unto you, and you have brought it to yourself by reaching out to their consciousness, whereas the person sitting next to you, standing next to you, who has not reached out, is

---

13. *The Heart of Mysticism: Volume 6, The 1959 Infinite Way Letters:* Chapter 7: July, "Spiritual Freedom."
14. John 12:32.

not in contact with it. And of course, the illustration of that is your radio. If your radio is tuned in to a station, you get what is on that station, but if you have a radio sitting right next to it that is not tuned in to that station, it may be just as good a radio, but it will not receive the program. The tuning in is the secret. Therefore, you go to the practitioner, make yourself a part of that practitioner's consciousness, and receive the light of wisdom, of spiritual truth, from that practitioner, and it becomes the law unto your affairs."[15]

IMPERSONALIZATION AND NOTHINGIZATION

Joel gave two specific practices that relate to spiritual healing: impersonalization and nothingization. The practice called impersonalization is one of the ways we practice the principle of the nature of individual being. The practice of nothingization is one of the ways we practice the principle of the nature of error. While Joel sometimes referred to impersonalization and nothingization as "principles," we will refer to them as "practices" because they are *actions* that we take to apply the principles.

Impersonalization

In Chapter 6, we set forth the idea that error is impersonal, meaning that evil is not *in* or *of* a person and does not arise *from* a person. Impersonalization puts that awareness into practice by separating the individual from the error or problem and recognizing that the individual is God in expression. Joel explains:

" Your first function in healing work is impersonalization. Remember that word, *impersonalization*. This

15. Recording 400A: 1961 San Diego Special Class, "The Essence of The Infinite Way, Part 1."

claim is not a person, not a condition, not a thing. It belongs to nobody. It is an impersonal activity or substance or imposition. We could call it the carnal mind or mortal mind. Use devil or Satan–whatever term you like–but impersonalize it. Take it out of the person. Realize that it isn't a person, it hasn't a person in whom to work. It is an impersonal claim of the universal mortal mind, the universal carnal mind."[16]

"The minute I recognize that God constitutes individual being, I must also recognize that no person contains within himself the source of any evil. There is no evil *in* anyone, no God-constituted evil and no self-created evil. Any evil that is manifesting *through* a person has its origin in what for lack of a better name may be called the universal carnal mind. To so dispose of it immediately separates it from the person, and leaves him as he originally was, the image and likeness of God, God Himself in expression, Life expressing Itself as individual being. There is then no evil in him: the only evil there is, is the impersonal evil inherent in the universal carnal mind. . . . The origin of the problem is not in the person and you cannot uncover the error in him because it is not there.

"The error is in a universal belief that there is a mortal man or that there is a condition or a creation apart from God. It is a *universal* belief, not your belief and not my belief. In the Infinite Way, this is called 'impersonalization,' and this principle is of primary importance in Infinite Way healing. No matter what the problem is, from corns to cancers, from an empty pocketbook to an empty relationship, it is not a person, and it is not in a person: it

---

16. *The Foundation of Mysticism:* Chapter 11, "Three Principles and Their Practice."

is a universal belief of a selfhood and a power apart from God. It is not the person because the person is God made manifest: he is Life expressed; he is Spirit revealed; he is the Soul of God incarnate. The very breath he breathes is the breath of God. He is really God-Selfhood. There is no evil in him, and there is no sin.

"Was it not at the trial of Jesus that Pilate said, 'I find in him no fault at all'[17]? That is exactly what our practitioners must say to every case: 'I find no fault in this patient, no fault at all, no evil. I find only that he is the Holy One of Israel, the child of God, the offspring of Spirit, the very life of God expressed.' This is impersonalizing the appearance."[18]

Nothingization

The practice of nothingization is the partner to the practice of impersonalization. It is a way to practice the principle of the nature of error.

"After the error has been impersonalized, there is a second step, and this is called 'nothingizing,' making nothing of it; in other words, realizing that God did not create the evil condition . . . The will of the Father is that we be healed of disease, that we be freed of lack, that we be forgiven our sins. Can these errors, then, be of God, and if they are not of God, do they have any power? If they are not of God, can they have any real existence?"[19]

---

17. John 19:4.
18. *Living Now:* Chapter 5, "God-Endowed Dominion."
19. ibid.

"When you are sure that you have impersonalized it [the error] so that you have absolutely no thought of the individual in your mind, then [nothingize it]. That means you have to go back to Genesis: 'God made all that was made, and all that God made was good. What God did not make was not made.'[20] Therefore, anything God did not make does not exist. And all that God made was good. If God made all that was made, and all that God made was good, then God didn't make a carnal mind, or mortal mind, or devil, or Satan. They have no existence except as mental concepts in the human mind.

"If you want to know how powerless a human concept is, close your eyes and build the biggest bomb you could possibly build. Build an atomic bomb and combine it with hydrogen and all the forms of nuclear fission you've ever heard of and multiply that by a thousand. Now throw it up here at me to see what it can do. Do you understand that? That's a mental concept. It has no substance; it has no law; it has no entity; it has no being. It only has form as thought. That's why you can see it in your mind, but you can only see it in your mind as a mental image.

"Once you begin to understand that all there is to the devil is an entity made in the mind of man, not in the mind of God, and that it has no law of God, no substance of God, no activity of God, no source of God, no avenue, no channel through which to work, you nullify it. You've recognized it for what it is: temporal power, the arm of flesh, nothingness."[21]

---

20. See Genesis 1:31.
21. *The Foundation of Mysticism:* Chapter 11, "Three Principles and Their Practice."

Joel says that practicing impersonalization and nothingization enables us to withdraw from the battle so that we do not fight evil, thereby obeying Jesus' great teaching, 'Resist not evil.'[22] But he says, "If we take out our mental sword and begin to deny and argue against the evil, or if we attempt to overcome some power, we are lost."[23]

In Infinite Way healing, we recognize that any appearance is neither *in* nor *of* the person and has nothing to sustain it.

> "It is necessary to know ... impersonalization and nothingization, meaning that the very moment any form of evil touches your consciousness, that you instantaneously realize, 'This is no part of person; this is the universal belief in two powers.' Then that you realize since that belief didn't come from God, it has no ordination. It has no law of God, no life of God, no substance of God, and it is a nothingness that you need not fear. Then rest in the assurance that God is omnipotence, omnipresence and omniscience."[24]

CAN ANYONE ATTAIN THE HEALING CONSCIOUSNESS?

Joel taught that every Infinite Way student who is committed to developing some measure of the healing consciousness can do so through dedicated, faithful, study and practice.

> "The healing consciousness is the consciousness that has the spiritual discernment to see through "this world" to "My kingdom." This discernment or ability to

---

22. Matthew 5:39.
23. *Our Spiritual Resources*: Chapter 5, "Spiritual Attainment Through Prayer."
24. Recording 376B: 1960 Melbourne Closed Class, "The Virgin Consciousness."

perceive Reality is not reserved for those who have had mystical illumination. It is possible for almost anyone who is willing to become a student of spiritual truth to attain a measure of spiritual discernment. There are those who achieve it in one day; there are those who achieve it in a few weeks or a few months; and there are others who work for years to achieve it. One deciding factor in the length of time it takes to develop this awareness is the desire for it.

"Spiritual discernment is not to be had for spare change or spare time. It requires a greater devotion than would be necessary in trying to learn a new language or to play a musical instrument. There must be the desire of the heart. Given that, and the willingness to study and practice, it will be only a short time before a person can achieve some measure of spiritual awareness and show it in actual work."[25]

" The healing principle of The Infinite Way is simple, but no one can bring about healings quickly just through *knowing* the letter of truth: it is *working with it* that develops this consciousness. It becomes second nature not to take in the appearance as if it were a condition, not to condemn a person, not to react to any appearance presented by a person, and that is when the healing consciousness is in full bloom, and then is when our healing ministry begins. Up to that time, we are practicing, practicing, and practicing to develop that consciousness. The consciousness that does not respond to appearances, the consciousness that is aware of the spiritual nature of creation and of the illusory nature of appearances, is a healing consciousness."[26]

---

25. *Awakening Mystical Consciousness:* Chapter 9, "The Mystic and Healing."
26. *Realization of Oneness:* Chapter 11, "Lifting Up the 'I'."

CHAPTER 10

MYSTICISM IN THE INFINITE WAY

Joel Goldsmith was a mystic. The Infinite Way is a mystical message, evidenced by the many book titles that point to the mysticism of the message: *Awakening Mystical Consciousness, The Foundation of Mysticism, The Heart of Mysticism,* and *The Mystical I.*

What is mysticism? This is how Joel defined it:

" The true meaning of mysticism is any teaching, any philosophy, or any religion that adheres to oneness with God. It is conscious oneness with God, the ability to receive impartations or guidance direct from God. It is the ability to commune with God, to be consciously at one with God, the ability to receive good from God individually and directly. We may sum it all up, then, in saying that mysticism is any teaching that brings out oneness with God, and this teaching of ours stresses, above all things else, oneness with God—conscious oneness with God."[1]

With that definition, it is easy to see that The Infinite Way is a mystical message.

---

1. *Consciousness in Transition:* Chapter 18, "Mysticism."

" The Infinite Way never had any intention of being anything but a mystical message, a message revealing the possibility of attaining its goal of conscious union with God, and the means of attaining it. During all these years, the writings and the recordings bear witness to this: The Infinite Way is not a system of attaining improved humanhood; it is the attaining of the Christhood."[2]

TWO PARTS TO THE INFINITE WAY MESSAGE

Although The Infinite Way is a mystical message, Joel identified two aspects to it—the "metaphysics" of the message and the "mysticism" of the message. He explains:

" Now, this message of The Infinite Way has two parts to it. One part is the letter of truth, which is a statement of the principles upon which this particular teaching is based. The second part of it is the mystical side, which is its meditation and demonstration of the presence of God."[3]

" The Infinite Way teaching is divided in two parts, its metaphysical teaching and its mystical teaching. The metaphysical part of the work consists of the letter of truth, that which you must know with your mind; that which you must study; that which you must practice. . . . This is the basis of that which follows [the mysticism] after we have perfected ourselves in this."[4]

---

2. *Consciousness Transformed*: September 14, 1963, "There Is Only One God Consciousness."
3. Recording 306B: 1960 Northwest Open Class: "Attaining Healing Consciousness Through Grace, Part 2."
4. Recording 270A: 1959 San Diego Special Class: "The Process of Infinite Way Healing and Its Principles."

" The metaphysics of The Infinite Way is made up of the letter of truth, and while studying that, it is natural that our human experience improves. Our health does get better, our living conditions, our business, human relationships, but that is not our goal. Our goal is the mysticism of The Infinite Way, that is, that part of the teaching that brings us into conscious union with God. That is our goal."[5]

Chapters 4 through 8 of this book address the realm of the metaphysics of the message because they focus on the principles and the practices.

Many people understand the word "metaphysics" to refer to the practice of using the mind as a power to achieve some effect. They believe that if you want a new home or a new car or a new relationship, you can get it by focusing your mental energy on that goal and using mental affirmations. But that is not the meaning of "metaphysics" in The Infinite Way. The metaphysics of The Infinite Way does refer to those aspects of the message in which you are using the mind, but the difference lies in the *purpose for which you are using the mind*. In the Infinite Way, we use the mind to learn, to contemplate the correct letter of truth, and to practice the principles. We do not use the mind *as a power* to bring about some material effect or some improvement to a human condition.

In Chapter 2, we said that The Infinite Way is a teaching, a way of life, and an experience. That "experience" of which Joel speaks is in the realm of the mysticism of The Infinite Way. Some say, "You can't teach The Infinite Way," but that is only partly true. The metaphysics of The Infinite Way—the correct letter of truth as reflected in the principles and the practices— certainly can be taught, as Joel did in his classes and writings. It

---

5. Recording 181A: 1957 Kailua Advanced Class, "Starting the Mystical Life."

is the mysticism of the message that cannot be taught because the mysticism is an experience that comes from within.

THE METAPHYSICS LEADS TO THE MYSTICISM

Joel emphasized that the metaphysical aspect of the message is the foundation for the mystical. He taught that as we eliminate erroneous concepts and replace them with the correct letter of truth, and as we engage in the practices, we are preparing to experience and live the mystical life.

" The mystical consciousness is developed through the metaphysical aspects of the Infinite Way, because in it [the metaphysics] there are consistent specific principles which develop consciousness."[6]

" When people do not know the letter of truth, the correct letter of truth, it is very difficult for them to acquire the spirit or consciousness that leads to the actual God experience. And so, the reading of the correct letter of truth, the study of it, the hearing of it, all these are steps opening our consciousness to a final experience."[7]

" What is the good of all this teaching? What is the good of all the years of study of these books?' And I will say to you that the Experience will not come without that. The study, the practice, the listening, and the reading are the steps that break down the mortal

---

6. *A Message for the Ages*: Chapter 9, "The Simplicity of the Healing Truth."
7. Recording 20B: 1953 New Hawaiian Series, "God as Law in Operation, continued."

sense in which we were born, that enable us to 'die' to mortal sense and to be 'reborn.'[8]

"To attain proficiency in first understanding, knowing, the correct letter of truth, then [proficiency] in its application to every phase of our human existence, until one by one these principles come alive in us, this then, opens the mystical center, and after that we need not live by taking thought."[9]

WHAT IS THE MYSTICAL LIFE?

In the mystical life, we live completely in the consciousness of God AS individual being. We no longer live from the human *sense* of being. We have realized our oneness with God, and we live and function in that reality. Good humanhood is not mysticism. In the mystical life, we live from "My kingdom," not from "this world." We take no thought. We do not even depend on statements of truth, because we have the full *realized* consciousness of Truth.

"The goal of the mystical life is for us to become beholders of God in action, where we ascribe nothing to ourselves—not even good motives. We no longer have desires. We no longer have needs. This is called 'living by Grace.' . . . If I prayed for something, it would mean I have a desire, an end, an object in life that I am seeking. But I have nothing to pray for. I have only this minute to live, this minute in which I must be fulfilled by the Spirit. . . . That is what the mystical life is—at-

---

8. *Beyond Words and Thoughts:* Chapter 1, "Toward the Experience."
9. Recording 262B: 1959 Hawaiian Village Closed Class, "The Mysticism and Metaphysics of The Infinite Way, Side One, continued."

taining that degree where every day you find yourself not wondering about tomorrow because there is no tomorrow for you; there is only a tomorrow for God."[10]

The mysticism of The Infinite Way refers to those aspects that are beyond thought, beyond the mental work of learning, processing, pondering, and practicing. When we are in the mysticism of The Infinite Way, we are dwelling in Christ Consciousness, or in conscious oneness with God, or Truth.

" 'Man shall not live by bread alone.'[11] Take that word 'bread' and think of it as meaning that man shall not live by his own understanding, his own experience, his own education, his own beliefs, convictions, or concepts. Man shall not live by his money, his investments, his business, or his capacity. Man shall not live by anything that has effect. Man shall not even live by the truth that he has learned out of books, but man shall live 'by every word that proceedeth out of the mouth of God.'[12]

"A dozen times a day the ear will be open, and into it will come guidance, direction, wisdom, and the experience of love, peace, joy, and dominion. You know that experiences are coming into your life which you, as a person, were never responsible for, things exceeding your own dreams.

"This is the meaning of the mystical side of The Infinite Way. It means to live no longer by the economy of the world, no longer by the traditions of the world, but always by an inner grace. Miracles have been wrought

---

10. *Living by Grace*: Chapter 5, "Living the Mystical Life."
11. Matthew 4:4.
12. ibid.

by the passage, 'My grace is sufficient for thee.'[13] Just think of replacing the 'I need money for this, that, or some other thing' with 'My grace is sufficient for thee in all things,' and let that grace take form in whatever way It will."[14]

Joel makes the point that all mystical traditions give the same message:

"It really makes no difference where we turn in the mystical writings: Persian, Moslem, Hindu, Chinese, or Japanese mystics, or the Christian mystics of the twelfth to the seventeenth centuries. They have all given the same message: *I Am*. That is the essence of mysticism, and when that realization is attained, it gives us freedom. Why? Because in that *I Am*-ness there is no longer a desire for anything or anybody; there is no longer an ambition; there is no longer any strife or any struggle. There is a resting in that realization. Then everything necessary for our fulfillment—whether it is a person, a place, a thing, a circumstance, or a condition—automatically flows into existence."[15]

If we think about the spiritual journey in three stages, we might say that in the first stage, we are in the consciousness of "God AND me." In the second, we come to the consciousness of "God WITH me." And finally, we enter the full realization of "God AS me." This is the mystical attainment.

---

13. 2 Corinthians 12:9.

14. *The Only Freedom:* Chapter 9, "Starting the Mystical Life."

15. *I Stand on Holy Ground:* Chapter 11, "Self-Purification, the Way to the Mystical Consciousness."

HOW DO WE ATTAIN THE MYSTICAL STATE OF CONSCIOUSNESS?

Joel taught that one attains the mystical consciousness in proportion to the degree of their dedication and practice. He knew that the work is to uncover or reveal the mystical consciousness already hidden within us, not to get something that we do not have.

"As long as you have the human mind and you are working with truth, what you are doing is you are having the truth destroy your human mind, your natural consciousness, and build for you, or unfold and reveal, disclose, to you this mystical consciousness which is hidden in every one of us. It is called the Son of God. . . . As we came into expression as an individual offspring of God, there was included in our being this mystical consciousness, which is hidden by the Adamic belief in two powers, and as long as we are entertaining this belief in two powers, our mystical consciousness remains hidden.

"Through our metaphysical and spiritual study and practice, the mystical consciousness comes into experience slowly, gradually, a grain at a time, so that in these preparatory years, what we are doing with the activity of truth in consciousness is really dissolving our mortal consciousness— 'dying daily' is Paul's term for it—and at the same time we are being reborn of the spiritual or mystical consciousness.

"The spiritual consciousness is being raised up in us, lifted up, unfolded to us, disclosed to us, until eventually there is enough of this mystical consciousness so that instead of living by the laws of matter, or even the laws of mind, we are beginning now to live by Grace instead of living by taking thought, even right thinking, even true thinking. . . .

"The entertaining of truth in consciousness—whether we read it, whether we hear it, or whether we are in the presence of those who have evolved a step ahead of us—all of this is the dying daily to our mortal consciousness and the being reborn of this spiritual center, spiritual consciousness, and the gradual taking over by it, until we come to Paul's statement, 'I live, yet not I.'[16] Now it is not I [the human, personal sense of myself] living. Now it is this mystical consciousness that is living *as* me. It goes before me. It prepares mansions for me. It performs that which is given me to do. It is the source of my bread, meat, wine, and water. It is the all-in-all to my experience."[17]

This mystical consciousness *is* the *I* that I truly am. It is my very Self. No other being or entity is "taking over" my life and living it. When I ascend to the mystical consciousness, I have realized my true identity and nature, and I am living as that; as my Self, the Self that I have always been, but of which I have been unaware.

"There is no new consciousness to gain, no other consciousness to seek; it is a purification of the consciousness which we now have which, in its purified state, is Christ-consciousness. In other words, after his illumination, Moses was still Moses, but with a purified consciousness. Jesus was still Jesus, but with that purified or Christ-consciousness. That is why he is called

---

16. Galatians 2:20.
17. Recording 407A: 1961 Chicago Open Class: "Mystical Consciousness."

Jesus the Christ, Jesus the enlightened. He is still the same Jesus, but now not unenlightened."[18]

To attain the mystical state of consciousness, we must persist in our dedication and practice, just as we must persist if we want to master anything.

"No matter how gifted an artist or writer or scientist may be, he still needs technical training. The Spirit flows, but the human mind brings it down into practical and workable experience. That is why, in the other realm [the material realm], there must be practice, practice and more practice. So, also, it is with us: the listening mind must become attuned to God. God reveals Itself to us, but we must constantly practice until that time comes when the Spirit so completely takes over that nothing is necessary in the way of conscious mental work."[19]

"The letter of truth is found in all Infinite Way writings, but it has not been understood by our students, nor has it been practiced by them even if or when they have understood it. They have given more attention to the mystical, inspirational side than, first of all, learning and practicing these specific principles until consciousness is developed.

"If Infinite Way students are to attain the mystical consciousness, it will come about through the study and practice of the principles which lead to a purification of consciousness.... The more these particular principles are practiced, the more Christ-consciousness is

---

18. *I Stand on Holy Ground:* Chapter 11, "Self-Purification, the Way to Mystical Consciousness."

19. *The Heart of Mysticism: Volume 2: The 1955 Infinite Way Letters:* Chapter 6: June, "Higher Views of God, Prayer and the Self."

developing in us, and the more of a transparency we are for the activity of the Christ. This is the mystical consciousness."[20]

As was said at the beginning of this book, attaining the mystical experience and the mystical way of life is the ultimate goal of the message of The Infinite Way.

" The consciousness which you are is already infinite, but day by day you are more aware of the infinite consciousness which you are. Infinite divine consciousness constitutes your being, and the life you are showing forth at this moment is the degree of the infinity which you are aware of at this moment. You may go still further to where you can say: 'He that seeth me seeth him that sent me.'[21] That would mean you have come into the realization of your divine Selfhood, your Christ-being in its totality. . . .

"Let your goal be a single goal—*illumination*—and there will come a day when 'that mind which was also in Christ Jesus'[22] will not be a quotation. It is your living mind by virtue of its character, essence, and nature. This is The Infinite Way *goal*—attaining that mind which was also in Christ Jesus—attaining illumination, attaining illumined consciousness—and grace will then descend upon you."[23]

---

20. *I Stand on Holy Ground*: Chapter 11, "Self-Purification, the Way to the Mystical Consciousness."

21. John 12:45.

22. Philippians 2:5.

23. *Consciousness Transformed*: August 31, 1963, "Growing Day by Day—Attaining the Transcendental Consciousness."

CHAPTER 11

A PLAN FOR STUDY

IT IS IMPOSSIBLE for me to convey the depth, the richness, and the beauty of The Infinite Way message as it unfolds under individual exploration, book by book and recording by recording. Each recording, each book, is replete with spiritual treasures that await discovery and promise extraordinary rewards to those willing to search. This book has barely scratched the surface, and if the message resonates with you or intrigues you, I cannot encourage you enough to begin exploring the books and recordings.

In Chapter 2, I said that this book was like a map, and that even if you have a good map of a city, you still must visit the museums, eat in the restaurants, and spend time at the historic sites and other attractions to fully experience the richness of the city. Likewise, to experience the depth and fullness of The Infinite Way message, you have to delve wholeheartedly into the wealth of books and recordings, and you have to consciously engage in the practices. If you want to explore the message further, this chapter suggests a way to begin navigating through the many resources available to you.

This book sets forth the premise and the purpose of The Infinite Way message and addresses the four major principles— the nature of God, the nature of individual being, the nature of error, and the nature of prayer. It describes the major practices and provides information about spiritual healing and the mystical life. As you begin to study the message, it can be helpful to keep this basic framework in mind.

For example, when you read a book or listen to a recording, you might ask yourself, "What principle is being discussed here? The nature of God? The nature of individual being? The nature of error? The nature of prayer? A combination? Or is this about one of the practices?" By doing this, you can preserve the core simplicity of the message, while ever expanding, refining, and deepening your understanding and insight. In other words, this book gives you the skeleton of the message, and through your reading, listening, study, and contemplation, you will put flesh on the bones.

The primary sources for studying the message of The Infinite Way are the books and the recordings.

INFINITE WAY BOOKS

More than fifty books capture the message of The Infinite Way. Two publishers are authorized by the Estate of Joel S. Goldsmith to publish the books in print and electronic versions. Acropolis Books is the primary publisher of Joel's written work, holding print publishing rights to all but four of the books. DeVorss & Company has the print publishing rights to the other four books. Acropolis holds the worldwide e-publishing rights to all the books.

You can find excellent detail for each book, including a description, the chapter titles, and a list of the source recordings used for the book, on the Joel Goldsmith Books website, which is sponsored by Acropolis Books at www.joelgoldsmithbooks.com, or on The Infinite Way Office website at www.joelgoldsmith.com.

To ensure that you are always working with the authentic books, be sure that you purchase books published either by Acropolis Books or by DeVorss & Company. They are the only two publishers authorized by the Estate of Joel S. Goldsmith.

The print versions of these authentic publications are available from Joel Goldsmith Books (www.joelgoldsmithbooks.com), from The Infinite Way Office (www.joelgoldsmith.com), and from many other book vendors. The e-book versions are available from Amazon, Barnes and Noble, and Apple. The Joel Goldsmith Books website provides links to vendors for the authentic versions of both print and e-books. In addition, Joel Goldsmith Books offers a subscription service that enables access to electronic versions of the entire collection of Joel's books.

Where to Begin with the Books?

Joel recommended that new students begin with these four books:

- *Living The Infinite Way*
- *Practicing the Presence*
- *The Art of Meditation*
- *The Art of Spiritual Healing.*

"Based on my own experience, I recommend that students begin their study with *Living The Infinite Way*, spend a couple of days on the Introduction, and then go on into the book. Following that, the student should devote two or three days to the Introduction to *Practicing the Presence*. Why those two or three days on the Introduction? Because it provides a foundation, explaining to the student the object of the book, what he is to attain, why he is to attain it, and giving him a reason for all that follows.

"To read books of this nature without knowing why or what the expected result should be is folly. All that happens when a student merely reads a book without understanding of its purpose is that he has read another book which was very sweet and pleasant to read, but nothing has been accomplished. After a few readings he should go back to the Introduction and ask himself, 'Did I get out of the book what its purpose is?' If not, he must go back again, because these books are not just to be read: they are books that are to be worn out until new copies are needed.

"Then I turn students to *The Art of Meditation* and *The Art of Spiritual Healing* and from there on, into any of the books in any order."[1]

We can add *The Infinite Way* to this list of recommended books. *The Infinite Way* is the first book that Joel wrote and throughout his ministry, he called it "our textbook."

" The whole basis of all my writing is in that one book [*The Infinite Way*], and sometimes I have taken one sentence out of that book and written a whole new book about it. Sometimes I have taken one idea and another whole book has come forth. That's the type of book *The Infinite Way* is. It's a book full of mystery, and it's a book full of surprises. It's a book that, once you think you begin to understand it, you read it the next time and find out that you missed a point entirely. It is the forever all-time textbook of The Infinite Way."[2]

The four introductory books and *The Infinite Way* provide excellent lessons on the nature of God, the nature of individual being, the nature of error, and the nature of prayer, as well as instruction on the practices and topics that are covered in this book.

---

1. *A Message for the Ages:* Chapter 11, "Guidelines for Spiritual Unfoldment Through the Infinite Way."

2. Recording 656B: 1956 Second Cape Town Closed Class, "Truth Is One."

Studying a Book

Often, new students are so happy to have found Joel's message that they read and read and read. This is fine, but at some point, it is important to really *study* the message. The dictionary says that "study" means "to apply the mental faculties to the acquisition of knowledge; to devote time and attention to acquire knowledge; to examine something very carefully; to investigate and analyze in detail; to read intently or meditatively; to reflect, muse, think and ponder."

As you have learned from this book, the ultimate goal in The Infinite Way is an *experience* of God. Yet Joel taught that study is the first essential step in the journey toward the experience:

" When one does not know the correct letter of truth, it is very difficult to acquire the consciousness which leads to the actual God-experience. So the earnest reading and study of the letter of truth are steps opening consciousness to the experience."[3]

It is helpful to have a method for studying a book that fits your own learning style. Some students like to read a chapter slowly, stopping often to ponder what has been read. Others quickly scan the chapter, and then go back and read it again with thoughtful consideration. Some take notes as they read, putting the message of the chapter into their own words, and later reviewing and contemplating their notes. Some find it helpful to capture the message of the chapter in a drawing, a poem, or some other art form. Find the study method that works best for you to ensure that you are truly **studying** the books and not just reading them.

---

3. *Living The Infinite Way:* Chapter 2, "Attaining the God-Experience."

Example: A Contemplative Study Tool

One study method that has proven useful for some students is using a "contemplative study tool." The idea is to contemplate specific questions after reading a chapter to ensure that you caught the message of the chapter. You can formulate any questions you like, but here is an example:

- What is the primary message of this chapter? How would I summarize the chapter in my own words?
- Which of the four major Infinite Way principles are addressed in this chapter? (nature of God, nature of individual being, nature of error, nature of prayer)?
- What new aspects of the principles did I learn?
- What practices were recommended or reinforced in this chapter that I can apply in my life?
- What new insights, revelations, or realizations came to me while working with this chapter?
- What questions do I have about the content of the chapter? You can always take questions into contemplative meditation, or you can research them using the Electronic Library Search Tool, which is described later in this chapter, or you can ask a fellow student or teacher for help.

A study method like this can be helpful for those who are new to the message. And, in keeping with Joel's counsel, when something in a chapter particularly catches your attention, it is always a good practice to stop and contemplate it. Another beneficial practice is to finish a study period with a time of silence and receptivity with the attitude, "I am listening. Reveal to me anything more I should know."

Infinite Way Letters

Joel said, "I always bring to light that the books of the Infinite Way Letters, however, are as important as any books we have, if not more so. Here in every chapter the student is introduced to certain principles and their application, so that he can always go to those books and find working tools."[4]

Joel sent a Monthly Letter to all Infinite Way students who subscribed to it. The twelve Monthly Letters from each year were then published collectively as a book. Joel treasured the Monthly Letter, saying, "If I had to give up all of The Infinite Way activities but one, the one that I would keep is our Monthly Letter. That Monthly Letter is a precious, precious activity, and for this reason: It is to keep us with a fresh message every month, a large enough message to last a whole month, but with specific principles for use and application in our daily experience."[5] He believed that by working with the Letters, students could keep their consciousness filled with truth and build their spiritual awareness.

Joel encouraged students not only to read the Letter, but to *study* it; to find the principles in it and to *apply* them in daily living so that they could make the message practical. He thought of the Monthly Letter as an "outline for study and practice":

"Too many people have received the letter and said, 'Oh, how beautiful,' or written me a letter: 'I think this is the best one you ever did,' all of which really means nothing, because unless they were able to find what was in that letter, and apply it in the practical experiences of their lives, the fact that it was beautiful, and the fact that it sounded wonderful, and even sometimes

---

4. *A Message for the Ages*: Chapter 11, "Guidelines for Spiritual Unfoldment Through the Infinite Way."

5. Recording 237A: 1958 Manchester Closed Class, "Spirit, Grace and Meditation."

poetic, really has no meaning. It is only when we catch a principle from the Letter, or two principles, and begin to apply them in our experience that the letter becomes of value."[6]

These are the books that were compiled from the Monthly Letters during Joel's ministry:

1954 Letters: *The Heart of Mysticism, Volume 1*
1955 Letters: *The Heart of Mysticism, Volume 2*
1956 Letters: *The Heart of Mysticism, Volume 3*
1957 Letters: *The Heart of Mysticism, Volume 4*
1958 Letters: *The Heart of Mysticism, Volume 5*
1959 Letters: *The Heart of Mysticism, Volume 6*
1960 Letters: *Our Spiritual Resources*
1961 Letters: *The Contemplative Life*
1962 Letters: *Man Was Not Born to Cry*
1963 Letters: *Living Now*
1964 Letters: *Realization of Oneness*

For many years, Lorraine Sinkler, the editor of Joel's books, worked with Joel to prepare the Monthly Letters. After Joel's transition in 1964, Emma Goldsmith, Joel's wife, asked Lorraine to continue publishing an Infinite Way Monthly Letter by drawing on the vast library of recordings of Joel's class work. Lorraine prepared the Monthly Letters through 1981, and the collections of those annual letters also became books.

Important Chapters

Joel identified specific chapters that were important for the serious student because they provided answers to the problems that most students encountered.

---

6. Recording 504A: 1962 Cape Town Class, "First and Second Meditations."

" I n order to build a consciousness of truth, all Infinite Way students should know the following passages as well as they know their own names:

'The New Horizon,' *The Infinite Way*

'God Is One,' *Living The Infinite Way*

'Protection,' *The 1955 Infinite Way Letters*

'Break the Fetters That Bind You,' *The 1958 Infinite Way Letters*

'Contemplation Develops the Beholder,' *The Contemplative Life*

'Introduction' and 'Love Thy Neighbor,' *Practicing the Presence*

'The Relationship of Oneness,' *The Art of Spiritual Healing.*"[7]

" W hy do I keep referring to those [chapters] over and over again? Because if you work with those specific writings, apply them to the problems of life that come to you in your own experience, ... if you work with them over and over, they will develop fourth-dimensional consciousness."[8]

Four of these chapters are in the four books that Joel recommended for new students, so if you read them, you can pay special attention to those chapters.

---

7. *The Contemplative Life*: Chapter 10, "Meditation on Life by Grace."
8. Recording 467A: 1962 "25" Private Group, "Leading up to 'Malpractice' and 'Anti-Christ.'"

INFINITE WAY RECORDINGS

The library of Infinite Way recordings includes over 1250 of Joel's class sessions. In Chapter 2 of this book, the section "Format of the Book" provides a detailed description of how these recordings are numbered and referenced.

Joel recognized the special value of a voice recording:

" S oon after the message of The Infinite Way reached the public through the writings, the call came for personal instruction, and that in turn led to the use of tape recordings. Through some electronic process, these recordings catch not only the words of the message, but actually the consciousness of the speaker. They convey to the hearer much more than the words themselves; they actually convey the spirit of the message."[9]

" E verything on these tapes gets on there as it is spoken, with no editing, no changing, no rehearsal, no recitation, just a spontaneous live message as it comes through. And as it's played back, it lives again, the same life that it has in going out of my lips."[10]

The Estate of Joel S. Goldsmith, represented by The Infinite Way Office in California, holds the copy protection on all these recordings. All recordings are available in CD and MP3 formats through The Infinite Way Office, and you can order them from the website at www.joelgoldsmith.com or by telephone at 1-800-922-3195. The recordings are also available in MP3 format through Apple iTunes. To ensure that you are always working with the authentic recordings, be sure that you purchase

---

9. *The Heart of Mysticism, Volume 5, The 1958 Infinite Way Letters:* Chapter 1, "Spiritual Unfoldment Through the Study of The Infinite Way."
10. Recording 195A: 1957 Second Halekou Closed Class, "The New Dimension."

them from The Infinite Way Office or from Apple iTunes, or that you subscribe to the Joel Goldsmith Streaming Service, described below.

Subscription Streaming Service

The Infinite Way Office offers online streaming access to the entire library of Joel's class recordings for a modest monthly fee. Using this service ensures that you hear the authentic recordings, with highest quality sound, sourced from the original reel-to-reel tapes. The service allows you to study in a serene, ad-free environment and provides many wonderful features that are helpful to a new student. For more information, go to www.joelgoldsmithstreaming.com.

Transcripts of the Recordings

Transcripts of all recordings are available from The Infinite Way Office at www.joelgoldsmith.com or by telephone at 1-800-922-3195. Some students find it helpful to read the transcript of the recording as they listen, so that they can highlight important passages or make notes.

Where Should a New Student Begin with the Recordings?

Some students like to explore the library of recordings and choose the ones to which they are drawn. For those who prefer a more structured study program, the list of recommended recordings below gives you a way to begin. These recommended classes have been specially selected for new students, and they elaborate on the topics covered in this book. Selections were made based on the sound quality of the recording, the completeness of the message in the class session, and their suitability for a new student. For each category, it is helpful to hear the recordings in sequence, but if specific recordings beckon you, feel free to listen to them first.

RECOMMENDED RECORDINGS FOR NEW STUDENTS

Overview: What Is The Infinite Way: Premise, Purpose, Principles, Practices

- Recording 103A: 1954 Seattle Closed Class, "The Infinite Way Reveals Your Relationship to God"
- Recording 103B: 1954 Seattle Closed Class, "The Infinite Way Reveals Your Relationship to God, continued"
- Recording 473A: 1962 Tulsa Special Class, "Beginning Steps on The Infinite Way"
- Recording 473B: 1962 Tulsa Special Class, "Continuing on The Infinite Way"

The Nature of God

- Recording 269A: 1959 San Diego Special Class, "The Nature of God"
- Recording 425A: 1961 Stockholm Closed Class, "Specific Infinite Way Principles and Practice"
- Recording 425B: 1961 Stockholm Closed Class, "Specific Infinite Way Principles and Practice, continued"
- Recording 261A: 1959 Hawaiian Village Open Class, "The Nature of God"

The Nature of Individual Being

- Recording 117A: 1955 Kailua Study Group, "The Deep Pool of Our Being"

- Recording 601B: 1951 Second Portland Series, "God, Substance of Individual Being"
- Recording 15A: 1952 Honolulu Closed Class, "The Nature of Individual Being"
- Recording 463A: 1962 Los Angeles Closed Class, "Son of God Raised Up"
- Recording 463B, 1962 Los Angeles Closed Class, "'I' Revealed"
- Recording 464A: 1962 Los Angeles Closed Class, "I Reveal Myself"

The Body

- Recording 59A: 1954 Chicago Practitioner Class, "My Identity—Body—Communion"
- Recording 102B: 1954 Seattle Practitioner Class, "Flesh and Flesh"
- Recording 513B: 1963 Princess Kaiulani Sunday Series, "Attaining Dominion Through 'I'"

The Mind

- Recording 496A: 1962 London Special Class: "Mind Is a Transparency"

Transition from Human to Spiritual

- Recording 442B: 1961 Hawaiian Village Open Class, "The Unillumined and the Illumined"

The Nature of Error

- Recording 280A: 1959 England Open Class, "The No Power"

- Recording 264B: 1959 Hawaiian Village Closed Class, "Living the Principles of Mysticism and Healing by Knowing Truth, continued"
- Recording 142A: 1956 First Steinway Hall Practitioner Class, "Above and Beyond Thought or Thing"

The Nature of Prayer

- Recording 343A: 1960 Holland Closed Class: "The Secret of Prayer—Release God from Obligation"
- Recording 468B: 1962 Chicago Closed Class, "Preparation for Prayer"
- Recording 460A: 1962 Los Angeles Closed Class, "Maundy Thursday and Preparation for Prayer"
- Recording 472B: 1962 Chicago Study Center Special Class, "Human, Metaphysical, and Mystical Prayer"

Spiritual Healing

- Recording 477B: 1962 Princess Kaiulani Open Class, "Infinite Way Healing Principles"
- Recording 275B: 1959 London Closed Class, "Treatment and Healing Work of The Infinite Way"
- Recording 203A: 1958 Adelaide Closed Class: "How to Heal"

Impersonalization and Nothingization

- Recording 346B: 1960 Manchester Closed Class, "Impersonalization of Evil"
- Recording 263A: 1959 Hawaiian Village Closed Class, "Three Principles and Their Practice"

Metaphysics and Mysticism of The Infinite Way

- Recording 292B: 1959 New York Closed Class, "Fourth Dimension"

Mysticism

- Recording 541A: 1964 Los Angeles Special Class, "Living the Mystical Life"
- Recording 554B: 1964 Seattle / Chicago Series, "Practicality of Mysticism"

Meditation, Including Practicing the Presence and Contemplative Meditation

- Recording 281B: 1959 England Open Class, "Practicing the Presence, Meditation, and Treatment"
- Recording 424A: 1961 Stockholm Closed Class, "Meditation—Its Function and Purpose"
- Recording 475A: 1962 Princess Kaiulani Open Class: "Ten Second Meditations"
- Recording 361B: 1960 New York Closed Class, "The Peak of Mystical Living"

Practicing the Principles

- Recording 413B: 1961 Manchester Special Class: "Building Transcendental Consciousness"
- Recording 476A: 1962 Princess Kaiulani Open Class, "A New Form of Practice"
- Recording 92A: 1954 Northwest Series—Portland, "The Practice of Truth"

Studying the Writings

- Recording 453A: 1962 Mission Inn Closed Class, "Special References for Study and Practice"

Studying Scripture

- Recording 391B: 1961 Maui Work, "Scriptural Quotation Lesson, continued"
- Recording 415B: 1961 London Open Class, "Scriptural Quotation Class on Supply"

SHORT EXCERPTS FROM CLASS RECORDINGS

If you would like to sample the recordings, you can listen to short excerpts from Joel's class recordings at https://www.goldsmith-global.org/audio-excerpts-from-joels-classes/. The excerpts address many of the topics in this book, including the nature of God, the nature of individual being, the nature of error, the nature of prayer, Christ, meditation, and spiritual healing. All class recordings are currently under copyright protection, and Goldsmith Global has posted these excerpts with permission and under a license from the Estate of Joel. S. Goldsmith.

OTHER RESOURCES FOR STUDY

Infinite Way Monthly Letter

The Infinite Way Office continues the tradition of sending a Monthly Letter to those who subscribe. The Letters are based on Joel's classwork. You can get more information from The Infinite Way Office website at www.joelgoldsmith.com, or you can call the Office at 1-800-922-3195.

Electronic Library Search Tool

The Joel Goldsmith Electronic Library Search Tool is a valuable resource for in-depth study of The Infinite Way message. It allows you to search for any word or phrase in a complete database of virtually all of Joel Goldsmith's books *and* the transcripts of his classes. The search tool can be helpful for studying a specific topic or for finding a specific reference. You can use the search tool to customize and deepen your study of Joel's work.

The search tool offers three search options:

1. Search books only
2. Search transcripts only
3. Search BOTH books AND transcripts.

The search results provide a list of the book titles and/or a list of the classes in which the search term appears, together with excerpts from the book chapters and/or transcripts that show some context for each instance of the search term. You can filter search results by a specific book or class to show only the instances of the search term in that book or class.

The search tool can be accessed from The Infinite Way Office website (www.joelgoldsmith.com), the Acropolis Books website (www.acropolisbooks.com), or the Joel Goldsmith Books website (www.joelgoldsmithbooks.com).

Online Study Group

My husband, Marty, and I host the Goldsmith Global Online Study Group (www.goldsmithglobal.org). It provides an opportunity for truth students around the world to meditate together and listen to Joel's class recordings in the context of planned study programs. The Goldsmith Global website is rich with study resources.

Many people who study or are interested in the message of The Infinite Way do not have a local group to attend. The online study group makes it possible to participate in a meeting using a computer, a telephone, or a mobile device.

The tape group is "live" in that all participants meditate together and hear the recording at the designated time. In this way, anyone, anywhere in the world can meditate with the group and experience the uplifted consciousness of the group meeting. Each meeting begins with a fifteen-minute meditation to prepare to receive the message of the day. Then the host announces and plays the recording. After the recording, there is a five-minute meditation to contemplate what was received in the message, and the meeting concludes. Details about the group and the study programs are on the website.

GODSPEED ON YOUR SPIRITUAL JOURNEY

There are many, many spiritual paths, and seekers who pray for light and guidance will be directed to the path that is right for them at each stage of their journey. As Joel said,

"Each one must determine the message that is right for him and who his teacher is. Do not think for a moment that everyone is going to derive the same measure of benefit from any and every teaching or teacher. There are some persons who respond naturally to the mystical teaching of the Infinite Way. That then becomes their path, and once they determine that this is their way, it is up to them to give it the utmost devotion that they have.

"For others, this may not be their path. That is why I am happy that in the Infinite Way we have never been led to form any kind of an organization; I do not want anybody held to this Way by membership. Everybody must feel free. If this message is not for you, keep on searching and seeking until you find the one that is. Do not think because somebody you know has had a beautiful healing in the Infinite Way or has benefitted from it that it necessarily means it is for you.

"Each one must have his teaching and his teacher, something to which he responds. Until he finds it, he must continue to search. When he finds it, something within him says, 'This is my way.' After that, he abandons all others and gives himself wholeheartedly to the one."[11]

The Infinite Way may or may not be your way, but you are always more than welcome to explore it freely and with no sense of obligation.

"In the message of the Infinite Way, each one is not only free when he comes to it, he is just as free when and if he goes. No one is ever bound to this message by membership, obligation, duty, or for any other reason, because this message recognizes above all that no person is seeking this message: he is seeking God-realization, and if this message can be a help to him on the way, he is welcome to it. It was the way in which I came, and it is set forth as a help for all those who may be led to it, but for no other reason. It is not to bind anyone ever in a membership, a duty, or an obligation."[12]

In that spirit of welcome, encouragement, and respect, I wish you bountiful blessings and Godspeed on your spiritual journey, wherever it may lead.

---

11. *Living the Illumined Life*: Chapter 11, "Teacher and Student on the Path."
12. *Living by the Word*: Chapter 4, "Easter, An Experience of Consciousness."

ACKNOWLEDGEMENTS

WITH UNBOUNDED LOVE AND APPRECIATION, I acknowledge my soulmate, husband, and partner, Marty, for his constant and loving encouragement, for the innumerable angelic ways in which he has facilitated this book, and for the light that he brings to my life each and every day.

To Sue Ropac at The Infinite Way Office and to Michael Krupp at Acropolis Books, I offer my sincere thanks for their gracious permission to use quotations from Joel Goldsmith's recordings and books, and for all they do to preserve the original message of The Infinite Way.

My profound reverence and deepest acknowledgment go to Joel Goldsmith, the enlightened master who shared The Infinite Way with us, to all the dedicated teachers and students who followed him and gave us "shoulders to stand on," and to all the Infinite Way students today who maintain the consciousness that sustains this remarkable and precious message.

Elizabeth Parker
Loomis, California

CPSIA information can be obtained
at www.ICGtesting.com
Printed in the USA
JSHW041300050722
27596JS00003B/127